NAMES OF THE BELIEVERS

NAMES OF THE BELIEVERS

JOHN KOESSLER

MOODY PRESS
CHICAGO

© 1997 by
JOHN M. KOESSLER

All Scripture quotations, unless indicated, are taken from the *Holy Bible: New International Version.*® NIV.® Copyright © 1973, 1978, 1984 by International Bible Society. Used by permission of Zondervan Publishing House. All rights reserved.

The "NIV" and "New International Version" trademarks are registered in the United States Patent and Trademark Office by International Bible Society. Use of either trademark requires permission of International Bible Society.

Scripture quotations marked (NASB) are taken from the *New American Standard Bible*. © 1960, 1962, 1963, 1968, 1971, 1972, 1973, 1975, and 1977 by The Lockman Foundation, La-Habra, Calif. Used by permission.

Scripture quotations marked (KJV) are taken from the King James Version.

ISBN: 0-8024-6179-4

1 3 5 7 9 10 8 6 4 2

Printed in the United States of America

For Mike Boyle,
Colleague and friend,
who gave me the idea.

CONTENTS

1
SALT OF THE EARTH

> You are the salt of the earth. But if the salt
> loses its saltiness, how can it be made salty
> again? It is no longer good for anything,
> except to be thrown out and trampled by
> men. (*Matthew 5:13*)

My father was a great fan of Dixieland jazz. Over
the years he amassed a sizable collection of
records and tapes featuring some of the greatest
artists of the '20s and '30s. I never acquired a taste
for his style of music, and one day when I complained about the "noise," he replied with a favorite
Latin phrase of his: *"Degustibus non disputandem est."*

When I asked him what it meant, he explained:
"It means, 'There is no point in arguing about
taste.'"

Jesus comments about what might be described as "tasteful Christianity" in Matthew 5:13.
Here, however, He is not speaking of aesthetic differences but about the critical role the church plays
in society. In referring to His disciples as "the salt of
the earth," Jesus is saying that Christians make the
world a habitable place. In other words, the only
reason the present world is livable is because the
church is still in it.

Today, when we refer to someone as "the salt of
the earth," we usually mean that he or she is a lik-
able person. But when Jesus used the phrase, He
was not talking about personality but moral character.

This comparison would not have seemed strange to Jesus' listeners because salt was an important part of their daily existence. Like us, the people of Jesus' day used salt as a seasoning to make food taste better. But during this time, salt's most important function was to preserve food. In New Testament times there was no plastic wrap or refrigerators to keep things fresh. If meat was to be kept from spoiling before it was cooked, it had to be cured with salt. When Jesus calls us the salt of the earth, it is a reminder that we are as important to the society in which we live as salt was to the homemaker in New Testament times.

Jesus' reference to salt would also have been familiar to the disciples because it was used by the rabbis, who compared the Torah, the first five books of the Old Testament, to salt, and said, "the world cannot survive without salt." By calling His disciples the salt of the earth, Jesus was saying, in effect, "You are the 'living Torah' to those around you."

It is no coincidence that this analogy appears in a context that deals with persecution. It anticipates that persecuted believers might be tempted to ask: "If the world doesn't want us, why doesn't God just take us home?" Jesus' answer is that the world, while it may not want the church, desperately needs its presence.

We should also note that Jesus includes a warning when He refers to His disciples as "salt." He is saying that there is a certain quality that is essential to the church, and without that quality, we become useless. The salt that was used by Jesus' contemporaries was not pure but a mixture of salt and other minerals. When it was exposed to air, it tended to lose its flavor and could no longer serve its original purpose. When this happened, the salt was sprinkled on walkways to prevent slipping, in much the same way we use rock salt today.

How does the church lose its saltiness? By conforming to the world around it. The church cannot function as salt when it conforms to the world it was meant to season.

There are times when it is good to conform. For example, when I am driving on the expressway, I don't want someone going south in my lane when I am traveling north. It is good to conform to the right things. Romans 8:29 promises that believers will be conformed to the image of Christ: "For those God foreknew he also predestined to be conformed to the likeness of his Son, that he might be the firstborn among many brothers." God uses my circumstances as I offer myself to the Holy Spirit to make me more like Jesus Christ.

Unfortunately, the conforming process can work in the other direction as well. Paul warns: "Do not conform any longer to the pattern of this world, but be transformed by the renewing of your mind. Then you will be able to test and approve what God's will is—his good, pleasing and perfect will" (Romans 12:2).

Who will shape us? Will it be God's Spirit, working through God's Word and our daily circumstances to transform us into the image of Christ? Or will it be the world, which presses us into its own mold? If we allow the world to shape us, we will become like flavorless salt, useless to God and man alike.

Being the salt of the world isn't always comfortable. Roger discovered just how hard it can be
when he moved into a flat in a rundown section of
Detroit. His upstairs neighbor was an unfortunate
woman who suffered from a mental disorder. Her
doctors had prescribed medication, but she usually
forgot to take it. Roger would often hear her
screaming at her husband all night long. Sometimes when she was finished with her husband, she
would come downstairs and pound on Roger's door
and scream at him.

During one of his neighbors' all-night family
fights, Roger heard the woman complain that she
didn't have enough money to buy food for the family. So the next day he went out and bought several
bags of groceries and left them at their door. The
woman took the groceries, but instead of thanking
Roger, she cursed him!

Perhaps you work with people whose values
are radically different from your own. Like Roger,
you may have an unfriendly neighbor. Or it may be
the members of your own family who have caused
you to plead with God that He change your circumstances. But instead of the changes you asked for,
things seem to remain the same. Now you begin to
wonder: "If God really loves me, why has He placed
me in such a situation?" Jesus' words provide the
answer: If the function of salt is to preserve that
which is decaying, where will it be needed most?

*Lord Jesus, make me more like You so that my in-
fluence in the world will leave behind the lingering
savor of Your presence. Amen.*

2
CHRIST'S CHURCH

And I tell you that you are Peter, and on this rock I will build my church, and the gates of Hades will not overcome it. I will give you the keys of the kingdom of heaven; whatever you bind on earth will be bound in heaven, and whatever you loose on earth will be loosed in heaven. *(Matthew 16:18–19)*

One bright June afternoon, a small crowd of friends sat in lawn chairs in our yard and watched as a team of workers built our new church. A prefabricated building, its walls had actually been made in a factory and then delivered to the building site on a large flatbed truck. Everyone cheered as the first wall swung into place, and in a few hours the entire frame was up.

The finishing process took much longer. Doors were hung and the inside walls were finished off with plaster, paint, and wallpaper. And after the builders completed their job, we turned our attention to the inside furnishings. We took as much care in deciding on the color of the carpet as we did in picking the building's floor plan.

However, before any of the walls went up, before one pane of stained glass was put in place, before an inch of carpet was laid down, or a single drop of paint was splashed on, the building's foundation had to be planted. Steel rods and concrete were used to fix the building's footings in place. Although this wasn't nearly as exciting as the raising of the walls, in many ways it was more important, because a building is only as strong as the foundation upon which it stands.

In Matthew 16:13–19, Jesus lays bare the foundation of His church in an exchange with the apostle Peter that took place near the end of His Galilean ministry. As the crucifixion drew nearer, Jesus began to focus less on the crowds and more on His disciples, in order to prepare them for His departure.

While traveling through the region of Caearea Philippi, Jesus asked the disciples to describe the rumors being spread about Him. "Who do people say the Son of Man is?" He asked. The disciples all spoke up at once. "Some say that you are John the Baptist come back to life!" exclaimed one. "Others think you are Elijah," said another. Someone pointed in Jesus' direction, chuckling, "Oh, really? I heard someone say that He was Jeremiah or one of the prophets." Everyone laughed.

In the silence that followed, Jesus probed His disciples further. "And what about you," He asked gently. "Who do you say I am?" The disciples looked nervously from one to another, as if they were afraid of giving the wrong answer. At last, Peter replied, blurting out the words like one who had been bursting to tell a secret that was burning inside him: "You are the Christ, the Son of the living God!" His eyes shown fiercely, daring Jesus to deny it.

But Jesus did not. Instead, He beamed back a smile of approval and said, "Blessed are you, Simon son of Jonah, for this was not revealed to you by man, but by my Father in heaven. And I tell you that you are Peter, and on this rock, I will build my church, and the gates of Hades will not overcome it."

Jesus' promise here seems to have been a kind of pun based on Peter's name. Peter's given name at birth was actually Simon, which meant "hearing." When Simon's brother Andrew first brought him to meet Jesus, the Savior renamed him Cephas, an Aramaic term that meant "stone" or "rock." The Greek form was *Petros,* or Peter. Anyone who knew Peter well could not help but see the irony in Jesus' words. Old impetuous Simon, the well-meaning but unstable fisherman. If his behavior as a disciple is indicative of his previous life, Peter was a man quick to speak and act, but easily swayed by the opinions of others. It was this trait that eventually caused him to deny his Lord and earn a sharp rebuke from the apostle Paul for shunning Gentile Christians when in the presence of Jewish believers.

However, Peter the man was not the rock upon which the church was founded. Rather, it was Peter's confession that Jesus Christ was the Messiah, the Son of the living God. It is here that we see the true foundation of the church and discover its most glorious name. The church that was about to come into being would not be Peter's church. It would be Christ's church, founded not upon human principles or earthly philosophy, but upon a personal relationship with the Creator of the universe. This church is made up of all those who recognize Jesus' true nature and genuinely confess Him as Lord and Savior.

This is an important reminder in an age when

so much of the church's thinking and practice seems to be drawn from the secular realm. In the world's view, an organization's first concern is efficiency: What is the bottom line? Are we making a profit? How can we get more for less? While efficiency is certainly important, the church's first concern is fidelity. For us, the bottom line is not the profit margin but the will of our Lord and Savior. Before we consider the methodology of others, before we even consider our own tastes, the church must look first to Christ.

It is in this name that we see the secret to the church's power. Jesus' words to Peter promised victory over the grave, giving a picture of the church storming the gates of Hades. This metaphor is used several times in the Old Testament for death (Job 17:16, 38:17; Psalm 9:13, 107:18; Isaiah 38:10). In the ancient world, a city's gate was its first line of defense. When an army seized the gate, it captured the city. Jesus pictured the church as an invincible army able to meet and overcome death in its own stronghold.

In Matthew 16:19 Jesus also granted the church authority to "bind and loose." The rabbis used these terms to speak of forbidding and permitting. Jesus characterized this authority as the "keys of the kingdom of heaven." In the ancient world, keys were a symbol of responsibility. For example, when Eliakim, the son of Hilkiah, was made governor of the palace under Hezekiah, the Lord prophesied: "I will place on his shoulder the key to the house of David; what he opens no one can shut, and what he shuts no one can open" (Isaiah 22:22). In Jesus' day, the scribes were given a key at their ordination to symbolize their possession of the key of knowledge (Luke 11:52).

The church, then, has real authority in the spiritual realm. While the prospects of individual congregations or denominations may rise or fall, the future of the church is assured. It will do more than merely survive; it will be victorious because it is built upon the indestructible foundation of Christ Himself.

Father, thank you for this reminder that the church belongs to Christ. Help us to recognize His authority and rely upon His power in all that we do. Amen.

3
FOLLOWERS OF CHRIST

> As Jesus went on from there, he saw a man named Matthew sitting at the tax collector's booth. "Follow me," he told him, and Matthew got up and followed him.
> *(Matthew 9:9)*

The French philosopher Voltaire was once challenged by a friend to ad-lib a story involving thieves. Voltaire thought for a moment and then began: "Gentlemen, there was once a tax collector. . . ."

Tax collectors were widely regarded as thieves in Jesus' day as well, a reputation that was often well deserved. Matthew's job before Jesus called him was to collect the tolls and customs due from those who brought merchandise in and out of Herod's territory. This task was assigned to the highest bidder, who then leased the responsibility to tax gatherers, lower officials who were responsible for actually collecting the money. These tax gatherers, or publicans, were allowed to keep any money that was collected over and above the promised amount. Some tax gatherers actually practiced a form of extortion by levying an amount that they knew could not be paid, and then charging high interest on the unpaid bill.

If being a tax collector was an unlikely career choice for Matthew because of its unpopularity, becoming a follower of Jesus the Rabbi was downright unimaginable. Matthew's friends provide us with a window into his lifestyle. They were primarily other tax collectors and "sinners," a technical term used in the New Testament for those who ignored the Torah and lived immorally. Jesus called Matthew away from all of this with the command to "follow me." The Greek verb used here meant to walk behind someone or to follow in their path. For Matthew, this was literally true. He "left everything" and immediately became a disciple of Jesus, traveling with Him from place to place (Luke 5:28). However, Jesus' invitation called for more than a change of residence. It also required a change of behavior. Matthew abandoned both a sinful lifestyle and a lucrative—but dishonest—livelihood.

This was not true of everyone who was given the opportunity to become a follower of Jesus. Some refused Christ's invitation to follow because of the uncertain conditions Jesus' disciples faced (Matthew 8:18–20). Others were unwilling to break family ties (Matthew 8:21–22). Still others were afraid of the financial loss they would incur as a follower of Jesus (Matthew 19:21). Although ultimately unwise in their decision not to follow, their estimation of the cost of following Christ was accurate. Jesus warned that those who wished to be known as His followers must be willing to say "no" to self and follow the way of the cross (Mark 8:34), and that they must make a daily decision to identify themselves with Him (Luke 9:23, 26). He said that their allegiance to Him must take precedence over every other human relationship: "If anyone is ashamed of me and my words in this adulterous and sinful generation, the Son of Man will be ashamed of him when he comes in his Father's glory with the holy angels" (Mark 8:38).

Instead of being ashamed of Christ, Matthew threw a large party for all his friends and made Jesus the guest of honor. A number of Pharisees were also there, probably not as guests but as observers, watching from the street. The Pharisees, whose name literally meant "separated ones," purposely avoided contact with the common people, or "people of the land," because they were not strict enough in their observance of the Law. In addition to the regulations found in the Law of Moses, the Pharisees were especially concerned about obeying the additional commands of the oral tradition that had been handed down to them by those who had interpreted the Law. A Pharisee would not confide in the common people or accept their testimony in court. In the Pharisees' view, the common people did not make suitable marriage partners because the Pharisees considered their women "unclean." In fact, the Pharisees taught that the "people of the land" were so unclean that it was unlawful even to eat with them. Consequently, when they saw Jesus not only associating with such people, but willingly attending a feast with tax gatherers and notorious sinners, they were outraged. When they asked for an explanation, Jesus replied: "It is not the healthy who need a doctor, but the sick. But go and learn what this means: 'I desire mercy, not sacrifice.' For I have not come to call the righteous, but sinners" (Matthew 9:12–13).

When John F. Kennedy was inaugurated as President of the United States, he electrified his audience and mobilized an entire generation with the challenge to: ". . . ask not what your country can do for you; ask what you can do for your country." Like President Kennedy's challenge, Jesus' call to His followers was one to serve. However, it is service grounded upon a different foundation. Normally, a leader looks for the most qualified candidates to be followers. But Jesus' choice of Matthew reveals a different agenda. He did not select His disciples on the basis of what they could do for Him but on the basis of what He could do for them. Because of this, the fundamental prerequisite for becoming a follower of Christ is faith.

As Christians, our confidence is not in our own suitability to the task, but in Christ's willingness to extend mercy to us. When we choose to follow Jesus, we exchange our lives for His, placing ourselves completely at His disposal. As Henrietta Mears has said: "God does not always choose great people to accomplish what He wishes, but He chooses a person who is wholly yielded to Him." It is this more than anything else, that will determine the kind of follower we become.

Lord Jesus, I accept the call to follow You and place my life at Your disposal. Empower me by Your grace to choose the way of the Cross each day and to introduce others to You. Amen.

4

THE BRANCHES

> I am the vine; you are the branches. If a man remains in me and I in him, he will bear much fruit; apart from me you can do nothing. (*John 15:5*)

When my son Andrew was four years old, he once came home from Sunday school clutching a small Styrofoam cup, into which he had lovingly placed a single marigold seed. The next morning he jumped out of bed, took the cup down from the windowsill, and immediately burst into tears. Alarmed, my wife, Jane, asked him what was wrong.

"There's no flower!" he wailed. "My teacher said that there was supposed to be a flower."

Jane explained to Andrew that it would take time for the flower to grow and that he would need to water it regularly and keep the cup on the windowsill so that it would get enough sunlight. He did, and sure enough, after a few days a small sprout had pushed its way through the dirt in search of sunlight. Soon, a tiny marigold plant was flourishing in Andrew's cup. It eventually grew so large that it had to be transplanted to the flower bed in front of our house.

Like my son with his marigold seed, we usually think of growth as something that happens automatically. To some extent this is true. The farmer plants the seed and waits patiently for the harvest. And we parents watch our children grow without thinking much about the process of physical development. But even in instances like these, certain conditions must be met before growth can take place. The farmer plants the seed, spreads fertilizer on the ground, and cultivates the plant. My children grow naturally, but the measure of their growth can be affected by their diet.

The same is true in the spiritual realm. In John 15:5, Jesus compares Himself to the vine and His people to its branches. The metaphor of the vine is used several times in the Old Testament to refer to God's people. In Psalm 80:8–9, the nation of Israel is compared to a vine transplanted from Egypt. The psalmist speaks there of the care God gave the vine when it was planted and describes how it flourished. The prophet Isaiah also compares Israel to a vine and describes how God prepared the ground, planted a choice vine, and watched over the vineyard.

Jesus takes this same metaphor and alters it slightly. According to John 15, Jesus is the vine and we are the branches. The emphasis on the importance of producing good fruit remains in these verses, but Jesus reveals the conditions that must be met before spiritual growth can take place. He tells us that the most important prerequisite for growth is that the branch must be connected to the vine (John 15:2). This illustrates that Jesus alone is the source of spiritual life. If we are not in Christ, that is, if we have never wholly trusted Him for eternal life, then we have no life.

In the natural realm, no matter how much water a farmer pours on a dead branch or how often he fertilizes the ground around it, the branch will never produce fruit. And regardless of how suitable the environment around us may be for spiritual growth, if we are not attached to Christ by faith, then we will derive no benefit from it.

The second condition Jesus emphasizes in these verses is that of abiding or "remaining" in Christ (John 15:5). While Christ alone is the source of our spiritual life, we bear a certain amount of responsibility for the degree of our spiritual growth. This is why we are commanded to remain in Christ in order to bear fruit. The New Testament word that is used here emphasizes relationship.

Jesus guarantees spiritual life, but He does not necessarily guarantee the quality of that life. Like physical growth, the measure of my spiritual growth is affected by how well I nourish myself. Spiritual nourishment, like physical nourishment, is determined by what I take in. And in order to abide in Christ, I must nourish myself on God's Word. "See that what you have heard from the beginning remains in you. If it does, you also will remain in the Son and in the Father" (1 John 2:24). As with the food I eat, this is something that must be done daily.

In addition to proper nourishment, we need exercise in order to be healthy. Exercise contributes to my spiritual health, just as it does to my physical health. I exercise myself in the Christian life when I take God at His word and obey His commands. If I obey Christ's commands, I remain or "abide" in His love (John 15:10). I can only do this if I realize that the power to obey comes from Christ Himself. I can do nothing apart from the power that He supplies (John 15:5).

Prayer is the third factor that affects my spiritual growth. Jesus promised that if I abide in Him and His words abide in me: ". . . ask whatever you wish and it will be given you" (John 15:7). In this respect, we have an advantage in our spiritual growth that surpasses its physical counterpart.

When I was in college, a girl that I was interested in stopped dating me because I was not tall enough. She had always dreamed of marrying someone who was over six feet tall. Hours of prayer could not have changed the fact that I was just two inches short of her standard. In the spiritual realm, however, I have often had growth spurts that were answers to prayer. Even in the best of conditions, my physical growth is limited by my heritage and genetic makeup. But in the spiritual realm, the full measure of Christ is my only limit.

Author and philosopher Ralph Waldo Emerson was so proud of his Massachusetts orchard that he spent many hours writing there and, whenever possible, received guests among its trees. He was proud enough of his skill in tending the orchard's pear trees that he sent a sample to the local agricultural fair and was soon rewarded by a visit from several members of a horticultural society. However, as he showed them around the orchard, Emerson discovered that it was not the trees that interested them, but the dirt. They wanted to know what kind of soil had produced such terrible specimens from so worthy a species of tree.

The point of this story is simply this: How well you grow depends upon where you are planted.

For the Christian, the most important prerequisite for spiritual growth is to be rooted in Christ.

Heavenly Father, help me to abide in Christ by continuing to study His Word and to obey. Enable me to grow to the full measure of the stature of Christ. Amen.

5
THE BELIEVERS

The apostles performed many miraculous signs and wonders among the people. And all the believers used to meet together in Solomon's Colonnade. (*Acts 5:12*)

When I was a young boy, it seemed to me that God ought to make it easier for me if He truly wanted me to believe in Him. One night, I decided to put Him to the test. "Dear God," I prayed, "if you are really up there, send me an angel." Then I closed my eyes and waited.

After a few moments, I felt sure that there was "something" standing next to my bed. My heart began to pound and my throat went dry. Terrified, I opened my eyes just a crack, not enough to see clearly, but wide enough to discern a large shape in the darkness a few feet away.

"Take it away! Take it away!" I prayed. "I didn't mean it! I don't really want to see an angel!" But when I finally got up enough courage to open my eyes completely, I could still see the shape. In fact, it was still there the next morning. But the bright sunlight revealed every detail of the pile of clothing that had been collecting on the chair next to my bed for the past few days. What I had taken to be an angel was really a pile of dirty laundry.

It is tempting to think that it would be easier to believe in God if He would perform for us the kind of miracles that He has for others in the past. Why doesn't He speak out of a burning bush or provide guidance by a pillar of smoke and fire? He could do that, but it wouldn't necessarily make people believe in Him.

God has, at times, chosen to confirm His Word with the miraculous. For example, Acts 5:12 says that the apostles performed "many miraculous signs and wonders among the people." Yet despite these miracles, some of which were quite spectacular, not everyone believed. The very miracles that drew some people closer to Christ seemed to have the opposite effect on others. In fact, when the religious leaders of that time saw the miracles performed by the apostles and noted that more and more people were listening to their teaching, they became so jealous that they arrested them (Acts 5:17–18).

The same thing happened in Old Testament times. The people of Israel saw many miracles during the Exodus, yet they still questioned God's ability to save after each one. Eventually, the Lord complained to Moses: "How long will these people treat me with contempt? How long will they refuse to believe in me, in spite of the miraculous signs I have performed among them?" (Numbers 14:11).

This lack of belief is not only true of miracles. Ordinary circumstances can have a similar effect. The same circumstances that spur one person into the arms of Christ will drive another further away. The difference between the two is a matter of faith. The thing that distinguished the early Christians from the others around them was not that they had seen miracles, but that they believed God.

Faith is the gateway to the Christian life. It is impossible to be a Christian apart from faith. The Bible says we are saved by grace, through faith (Ephesians 2:8). This means that when we place our trust in Jesus, we are instantly joined to Him. Martin Luther wrote that the chief article and foundation of the gospel is that one must recognize Christ as a gift before holding Him as an example. It is no use trying to be *like* Christ until we are *in* Christ, and the only way to be in Christ is to accept the invitation to believe in Him as God's Son and our Savior.

The Bible tells us that faith is a matter of believing what has been written. Jesus attributed the unbelief of the religious leaders of the time to the fact that they could not believe what had been written about Him in the Scriptures: "If you believed Moses, you would believe me, for he wrote about me. But since you do not believe what he wrote, how are you going to believe what I say?" (John 5:46–47).

The Bible also tells us that faith is a matter of believing what has been seen. Jesus said: "Do not believe me unless I do what my Father does. But if I do it, even though you do not believe me, believe the miracles, that you may learn and understand that the Father is in me, and I in the Father" (John 10:37–38).

Faith is the ruling principle in the Christian life. Unlike the training wheels that helped to steady me when I rode my first real bicycle, I will never outgrow my need for faith. The Christians in Galatia made the mistake of thinking that faith was only for "beginners," and they were reproved by the apostle Paul: "I would like to learn just one thing from you: Did you receive the Spirit by observing the law, or by believing what you heard? Are you so foolish? After beginning with the Spirit, are you now trying to attain your goal by human effort?" (Galatians 3:2–3).

The Bible is clear that we need real faith in order to receive salvation. It is also clear that faith is believing what has been written and what has been seen. We must not, however, confuse faith with emotion. Oxford professor C. S. Lewis, in his book *Mere Christianity,* observed that our moods, unlike genuine faith, are subject to change: "Now that I am a Christian, I do have moods in which the whole thing looks very improbable: but when I was an atheist I had moods in which Christianity looked terribly probable." The real value of faith, Lewis explained, is that it tells your shifting moods "where they get off."

Someone has said that faith is believing in God when common sense tells you not to. The Bible, on the other hand, defines faith as ". . . being sure of what we hope for and certain of what we do not see" (Hebrews 11:1). Faith is actually *uncommon sense:* insight granted by the Holy Spirit and based upon truth. According to one of his friends, it was this kind of faith that enabled Oswald Chambers, the great Scottish evangelist and author, "to see angels where I saw only a fence."

Would it have been easier for me as a child to believe if God had allowed me to see an angel or performed some miracle in my bedroom that night? Probably not. The record of biblical history shows that it takes the eyes of faith, not the witnessing of miracles, to correctly interpret the works of God. If I could not accept what had already been written of Jesus or perceive the truth in what Christ had already done, a new work from God would not have helped me. The angel would be there, but I would have seen only a pile of clothes.

Holy Spirit, grant that I might see with the eyes of faith. Help me to believe what has been written about Christ in Your Word and to take to heart the testimony of what Christ has done. Only then will I be able to see Your hand in all that I do. Amen.

6
THE DISCIPLES

In those days when the number of disciples was increasing, the Grecian Jews among them complained against the Hebraic Jews because their widows were being overlooked in the daily distribution of food. *(Acts 6:1)*

Mark Twain made this observation about his experience of learning to become a river boat pilot in his book *Life on the Mississippi:* "Two things seemed pretty apparent to me. One was, that in order to be a pilot a man has got to learn more than any one man ought to be allowed to know; and the other was, that he must learn it all over again in a different way every twenty-four hours."

Jesus' followers would probably have said something very similar to that. They were known as "disciples," a term that literally meant "learners." The rabbis of Jesus' day attracted followers who placed themselves under the authority of their teachers. One who became a disciple made a personal commitment to the rabbi he followed. These disciples studied the rabbi's teaching, compared it with the teaching of the Torah, and eventually passed it on to others who became their disciples.

Jesus' method of discipleship followed a similar pattern. His disciples lived with Him and memorized His instruction. They traveled with Him from place to place and passed down what they had learned to others (2 Thessalonians 3:6).

Yet in many ways, Jesus' approach was radically different from His contemporaries. While the rabbis accepted only the most promising students, many of Jesus' disciples would hardly have seemed like worthwhile candidates. For example, unlike the religious teachers of His day, Jesus welcomed women as His disciples and allowed them to learn at His feet along with the men (Luke 10:38–42).

Another distinctive of Jesus' methodology was His hands-on approach to training. Instead of merely passing down the tradition of the teachers who went before Him, Jesus gave His disciples a fresh perspective on the truth of God's Word and coupled His teaching with practical opportunities to implement what He taught. Failure was part of the disciples' training! Jesus often assigned them tasks, knowing in advance that they would not always be successful in their attempt to complete them. He used their mistakes to teach them important lessons. The most obvious example of this was the apostle Peter's denial of Christ. Jesus predicted that Peter would deny Him three times and then urged: ". . . when you have turned back, strengthen your brothers" (Luke 22:32).

The events described in Acts 6:1–6 show that this learning process continued even after Christ ascended into heaven. It didn't take long for the newly formed church to encounter its first internal conflict. As its numbers increased, the cultural differences between those who had adopted the language and customs of Greek culture and others who held on to the language and customs of Hebrew culture became more apparent. They were looked down upon by those who considered such practices a form of religious compromise. The fact that these more-conservative believers spoke only Aramaic created an additional barrier. And soon the Greek-speaking Christians came to the apostles complaining that the needs of their widows were being overlooked.

This should encourage us for several reasons. First, it shows that these same believers who were able to have such a profound impact on their own generation faced problems similar to those that we struggle with today. Like today's believers often do, they misunderstood one another and had interpersonal conflicts. And if Christ was able to use them despite their weaknesses, He can do the same with us.

Secondly, the disciples offer a helpful reminder that conflict is a normal part of the church's growth and development. Numerical growth created obstacles on several fronts for the early church. It created logistical problems as the number of people with needs grew beyond the limits of the church's organizational structure. It also created interpersonal conflicts when new members did not automatically bond with those who were already part of the church. In fact, the believers at Jerusalem seem to have divided themselves into distinct "cliques" that fell along ethnic lines.

Numerical growth, like physical growth, is always accompanied by growing pains. New members must be assimilated and old organizational structures must be modified. The church's dreams and plans must undergo a subtle change as newcomers add their input. Sadly, many churches respond to this traumatic experience by sabotaging their own growth. Like the Jerusalem church, they "stick to their own" and refuse to make a place for new attenders. They may hold on to the reigns of power and not allow newcomers to exercise significant influence in the church's decision-making process.

The apostles' response to this first crisis enables us to see where their priorities lay. Peter explained, "It would not be right for us to neglect the ministry of the word of God in order to wait on tables" (Acts 6:2). Although Peter's words may give the impression that he regarded this as a trivial problem, his solution shows that he was well aware of its critical nature. So he asked the church to choose seven responsible people to oversee its ministry to those widows who were being neglected.

It is not surprising that all the names of those who were selected are Greek in origin, since the complaint originally arose among the church's Greek-speaking believers. A split along ethnic lines this early in the church's development would have left it hopelessly fragmented. What is more, it would have greatly hindered the church's eventual outreach to the Gentiles. It is very possible that one of God's purposes in allowing the church to endure this conflict was to help it prepare for the eventual inclusion of the Gentiles. In fact, one of the seven who was chosen was Nicolas, a convert from Antioch, the place where the gospel was first preached to the Gentiles (Acts 11:19–20).

When the disciples confronted the apostles with the problem, Peter resisted the temptation to "micro-manage" the situation. Instead of attempting to resolve it personally, he wisely delegated this important ministry to others. This left the apostles free to devote themselves to prayer and the ministry of the Word.

The qualifications listed by Peter for those to be selected were spiritual in nature. They were to be believers whose lives showed evidence of being "full of the Spirit." The apostles were not looking primarily for administrators so much as for disciples. This stands in stark contrast to the approach taken by many churches today. Too often, church offices are filled by candidates who have been selected on the basis of popularity, financial success, or political clout. The choice of the seven reveals to us that spirituality ought to be a factor, even in those ministries that do not seem to be overtly spiritual in nature.

What happened as a result of these changes? According to Acts 6:7, ". . . the word of God spread. The number of disciples in Jerusalem increased rapidly, and a large number of priests became obedient to the faith." Because its members continued to be learners, the early church was able to handle its growth successfully. Its secret was to remain focused on God's Word, dedicated to prayer, and sensitive to the leading of the Holy Spirit in their decisions and appointments to service. They weren't perfect; they were just disciples.

Holy Spirit, help us to be sensitive to Your leading as we fulfill our own ministries and appoint leaders in our churches. Place within us the heart of a learner, a heart that is willing to grow and adapt in each new situation. Amen.

7

ABRAHAM'S OFFSPRING

> Therefore, the promise comes by faith, so that it may be by grace and may be guaranteed to all Abraham's offspring—not only to those who are of the law but also to those who are of the faith of Abraham. He is the father of us all. *(Romans 4:16)*

Nineteenth century British Prime Minister William Gladstone was visiting an antique shop and came across a painting of a seventeenth century aristocrat. He liked the painting so much that he nearly bought it, but after long deliberation finally decided that the dealer was asking too much for it. Later, while admiring the paintings of a wealthy London merchant whose home he was visiting, Gladstone was surprised to see the very same portrait hanging on the wall. "Do you like it?" the merchant asked. "It's a portrait of one of my ancestors, a minister at the Court of Queen Elizabeth." "Three pounds *less*," Gladstone replied, "and he would have been my ancestor."

Gladstone's witty response to his guest points out a very simple fact: We can't choose our ancestors. No matter how wealthy or influential we are, we can't change our family background. But if you could select your own ancestors, would you choose Abraham? Born in Mesopotamia, Abraham moved from the city of Ur to Haran, a town about fifty miles east of Carchemish. This, however, was only the first stop on a lifelong journey that would make Abraham the Bible's prototypical pilgrim.

While still living in Ur, Abraham heard God's call to leave all that was familiar—his homeland and his countrymen—and go to a land that God would show him. Abraham had no map. He had no travel brochures. There were no airports or automobiles to speed the journey. But Abraham obeyed God's command, and at the age of seventy-five, Abraham set out with his wife, servants, and even his nephew Lot, counting on God's promise to make him into a great nation (Genesis 12:1–3). Although God had promised to give Abraham the land to which he was traveling, he lived there like a stranger in a foreign country, leading the life of a Bedouin tribesman (Hebrews 11:9).

Abraham became a wealthy man during his travels but lacked the one thing that he desired the most. "O Sovereign Lord," he complained, "what can you give me since I remain childless and the one who will inherit my estate is Eliezer of Damascus?" (Genesis 15:2). The Lord then appeared to Abraham in a vision and promised to give him more descendants than could be counted. And the Bible says that Abraham, ". . . believed the Lord, and he credited it to him as righteousness" (Genesis 15:6).

By the time Abraham was in his nineties, his wife, Sarah, still had not given birth to any children. Her womb was barren, and Abraham was "as good as dead" (Hebrews 11:11–12). When Abraham had reached the age of ninety-nine, the Lord reaffirmed His promise, and Sarah, who could only laugh in disbelief, became pregnant a short time later. When Sarah gave birth to her first son, they named him Isaac, which meant "laughter."

Abraham's dream had come true, but the test of his faith was only beginning. Some time after Isaac was born, the Lord came to Abraham again with an incredible request: "Take your son, your only son Isaac, whom you love, and go to the region of Moriah. Sacrifice him there as a burnt offering on one of the mountains I will tell you about" (Genesis 22:2). Abraham once again found himself traveling to an unknown location. This time, however, it was not to receive his inheritance, but to sacrifice it on an altar.

There is no record of any discussion over the matter. God did not explain His purpose and Abraham did not argue with the command. He took the wood for the burnt offering, a knife, and the son he loved more than his own life. He bundled the wood on his son's back, and the two started up the mountain.

In childlike simplicity, Isaac asked his father about what was to take place: "The fire and wood are here, but where is the lamb for the burnt offering?" Abraham's reply reflected a similar trust. "God himself will provide the lamb," he explained. Did Abraham know that God never intended to allow him to carry out the sacrifice? Probably not. He knew only that God had promised to raise up a line of descendants through his son: "Abraham reasoned that God could raise the dead, and figuratively speaking, he did receive Isaac back from death" (Hebrews 11:19). As Abraham lifted the knife to carry out the awful command, God spoke from heaven.

"Abraham! Abraham!" He cried.

The old man choked back a cry of relief, as the knife fell from his shaking hand.

"Here I am," he gasped.

"Do not lay a hand on the boy," God said. "Do not do anything to him. Now I know that you fear God, because you have not withheld from me your son, your only son."

Blinking back the tears, Abraham saw a ram caught by its horns in a nearby thicket. It was the ram, chosen and provided by God, that died in Isaac's place that day.

It was not Abraham's actions that set him apart from others of his day, but his faith. His remarkable behavior was merely a reflection of his confidence that God would follow through on what He had promised. It is true Abraham had his moments of doubt. There were occasions when he tried to take matters into his own hands and accomplish by his own power what God alone could do. But each time, he learned his lesson. The general tenor of Abraham's life was one of faith, and he was accepted by God because he believed.

The same must be true of us. The promise of forgiveness in Christ comes only by faith. Those who accept God's offer follow in the path of their pilgrim father Abraham. They become his descendants, heirs to the title "friend of God," and brothers with Christ. All are descendants in faith of a heritage that cannot be purchased at any price, but must be received as a gift.

God of Abraham, thank You for the example of Your servant Abraham. I pray that I might be as firm in my belief and as quick in my obedience as he was. By grace and through faith in Your Son, I name You as my friend. Amen.

8

THOSE WHO HAVE BEEN BROUGHT FROM DEATH TO LIFE

> Do not offer the parts of your body to sin, as instruments of wickedness, but rather offer yourselves to God, as those who have been brought from death to life; and offer the parts of your body to him as instruments of righteousness. *(Romans 6:13)*

In the 1970s a popular bumper sticker read: "Today is the first day of the rest of your life." For people like Ray, this is literally true. Seriously ill with cancer a few years ago, some thought that he might die. Now healthy, each sunrise is an unexpected gift to Ray. "It is amazing how your perspective changes when you are dying," he explains. "You begin to appreciate the smallest effort."

Recently, a young woman who feared that she might also have cancer made a similar observation to me: "I used to like to shop for antiques. Now I think, 'What if you are dying? Isn't there something better you could be doing with your time? This is just someone else's junk.'"

The approach of death often changes the way we view our actions. The things that seemed so pressing before are now easily shelved. The objectives that appeared so worthwhile a short time earlier now look trivial and foolish. This change of perspective is what some of the older writers meant when they spoke of the ability to "die well." Jeremy Taylor, the seventeenth century Anglican bishop who wrote the classic work *Holy Dying,* noted that God is remarkably frugal with time: "He has scattered the sky with stars like a gardener scattering grass seed over a lawn. He has made an incredible variety of animals. He has provided us a wide choice of food and drink, even though a very few would have kept us alive. Yet God parcels out time carefully, drop by drop."

When we suddenly realize that we have reached the limit of the moments apportioned to us by God as our share of this life, every deed becomes precious. The seconds, once carelessly squandered, now come under close scrutiny. The value of each one is carefully weighed in the balance, like the miser trying to extract the last few motes of gold dust from the bottom of his bag.

In this verse, the apostle Paul asks for a similar transformation of our perspective, but for a very different reason. We are to evaluate every thought, word, and action, not because we stand at the end of life, but because we are poised like runners at the beginning. "Offer yourselves to God," he urges, "as those who have been brought from death to life."

Sadly, there are many Christians today who are ready to die but unprepared to live. They know only that Jesus Christ has assured them a place in heaven. But what they don't realize is that this heavenly reality also has earthly implications. The Bible tells us that those who have trusted in Christ have died with Christ. As Paul puts it, they are "dead to sin, but alive to God in Christ Jesus" (Romans 6:11). They have been given far more than "a new lease on life." Through the power of the Holy Spirit, they have a new life principle at work in them. As a result, they no longer have to let sin reign in their lives.

In effect, Paul says that once we are in Christ we are no longer compelled to allow the sin principle to function like a king in our lives. Very few kings hold absolute power today, but in biblical culture, the king's word was to be obeyed. Prior to my coming to faith in Christ, sin functioned similarly. Sin was the ruler and I was its servant. I did not always like its directives, but there was little that I could do about them.

Sin is a cruel monarch and knows nothing about moderation in its treatment of those who serve it. When sin reigns, it reigns to the point of death (Romans 5:21). The apostle's point is that through the cross we have shifted our allegiance to a new master. When we come to Christ, we are to offer ourselves as servants to God and the parts of our body as instruments of righteousness.

There is an important order in this command. Before we offer the parts of our body in service, we must first offer ourselves to God "as those who have been brought from death to life." It has been said that some of the slaves who were freed from slavery after the Civil War continued to live with their old masters and serve them. They did so because they knew of no other way of life. The same can be true in the spiritual realm. We must know what we are *in Christ* before we can know what to do *for Christ*. I can not offer my body in service to God if I do not understand that I have been given a new ability to do so.

The Greek word that is translated "instrument" literally means "tools." When we place ourselves at

God's disposal, we become tools of righteousness. Otherwise, we are tools of sin and death. Interestingly, this same word can also be translated "weapon." In God's hands, we become weapons of righteousness. But we can also become weapons of sin.

Once, while helping a former missionary clean out his basement, I came across an old spear. I was impressed by its smooth lines and deadly point. As I hefted it, I felt its balance and imagined how it must have been used in the hands of its original maker. Perhaps it was used to supply meat for the tribe or to defend against its enemies. In the hands of the wicked, it might even have been used for evil purposes. But there in the basement it served neither purpose, existing only as a curious artifact in an alien culture.

This can never be true of those who are in Christ. Like it or not, we are either the instruments of God or instruments of sin. If we are not placing ourselves in the hand of our Redeemer as weapons of righteousness, then we are weapons of death.

Ray's brush with death fundamentally changed the way he looked at the remainder of his life. At times, it made him impatient for that life to be over. When I mentioned to him that there were times when, even as a Christian, I struggled with the fear of death, he chuckled and said: "I have the opposite problem."

"What do you mean?" I asked.

"I have been to the edge of the abyss and seen what's on the other side," he explained, smiling. "Sometimes I can't wait to die."

I was surprised that Ray would say that. He certainly did not live like someone who was waiting to die. It seemed to me that he utilized every minute for the kingdom, placing himself at Christ's disposal. But, like the apostle Paul, my friend was caught between two longings. Drawn by the desire to depart and be with Christ, which is far better, but eager to be used by God while he remained in this world (Philippians 1:23).

Would the apostle Paul agree with the old writers who said that it was more important to know how to die well? I don't think so. I believe that he would say that as important as it is to know how to die, it is even more important to know how to live. Especially for those who have been brought "from death to life."

Risen Christ, I thank You for giving me new life by Your death and resurrection. Show me how to use the moments You have apportioned to me, so that each one will contribute to Your glory. Amen.

9
CHILDREN OF GOD

> The Spirit himself testifies with our spirit that we are God's children. Now if we are children, then we are heirs—heirs of God and co-heirs with Christ, if indeed we share in his sufferings in order that we may also share in his glory. (Romans 8:16–17)

John never questioned who his father was. All he had to do to verify the answer was to look in the mirror. Ever since he was a small boy, everyone had told him that he was the "spitting image" of his dad. After he was married and had children of his own, John came across a picture of his father as a young man and showed it to one of his sons. "Who do you think this is in the picture?" he asked. His son looked at the image in the photograph for a moment and then smiled suspiciously, wondering if John was trying to play some kind of a trick. "It's you, Dad," his son said. "Who was I supposed to think it was?"

Sean's case is different. The fact that he resembles his parents physically is purely coincidental. Sean was adopted. Still, it isn't hard for him to call his adoptive parents "Mom" and "Dad." He has daily proof that they are his parents in the loving way that they care for him. And he also has it in writing. Sean's parents have the papers to prove their love for him. If someone were to suggest that a blood relationship might make a difference in their feelings for their son, they would be quick to point out that they became Sean's parents by choice. No one forced them to adopt him.

Those who have placed their faith in Jesus Christ are more like Sean than John. They belong to God by adoption. Galatians 4:5 tells us that God's purpose in sending Jesus Christ into the world was "that we might receive the full rights as sons." Romans 8:15 in the King James Version even refers to the Holy Spirit as "the Spirit of adoption."

In Greek and Roman culture, adoption was initiated by the father—usually to provide himself with an heir—and was often accompanied by the making of a will. A similar practice existed in Hebrew culture, as is seen in Scripture. Abraham adopted his servant Eliezer of Damascus (Genesis 15:2). Moses was adopted by Pharaoh's daughter (Exodus 2:10). After her parents died, the Old Testament heroine Esther was adopted by her cousin Mordecai (Esther 2:7).

The most important example of this practice in the Old Testament, however, was God's choice to adopt the nation of Israel. In Romans 9:4, the apostle Paul includes "the adoption as sons" in his list of Israel's privileges. When God called Israel out of Egypt, He referred to the fledgling nation as "my firstborn son" (Exodus 4:22–23). God also used the language of adoption when He entered into a covenant with David and promised to establish his throne forever (2 Samuel 7:13–14).

What was true on a national level for Israel has now become a personal reality for those who are in Jesus Christ. Through faith in Christ, we have been given the right to address God as Father. Because of

this, an important part of the Holy Spirit's ministry
is to provide us with the assurance that we are children of God. Romans 8:15 says that through the
Holy Spirit, we find the confidence to address God
as "Abba," an Aramaic term that is roughly equiva-
lent to the term *Daddy,* or *Poppa.* According to the
Talmud, "Abba" was one of the first words spoken
by a child. It was used as a term of endearment, but
only by family members. No slave or servant would
have referred to the head of the house as "Abba."

Adoption into God's family brings with it both
reward and responsibility. As children of God, we
have become heirs of God and co-heirs with Christ.
As co-heirs with Jesus, we share in the inheritance
that is coming to Christ, one that Christ Himself
has guaranteed for us. But what exactly is it that we
will share with Christ?

We will share His life (Matthew 19:29). By dying on the cross, Jesus Christ became the "source of
eternal salvation" for us (Hebrews 5:9). Through
the Holy Spirit, He makes that life available so that
our daily actions reflect the fact that Christ is living
through us (Galatians 2:20).

We will share His kingdom (Matthew 25:34).
Christ promised those who followed Him that they
would also rule in His kingdom. Christ's work has
made us qualified "to share in the inheritance of the
saints in the kingdom of light" (Colossians 1:12).

We will share in His glory. Because we have
been given a new status as God's children, we have
access to our heavenly Father and "rejoice in hope
of the glory of God" (Romans 5:2).

We will share in Christ's likeness. We know
relatively little about what life will be like in Christ's

presence, but we do know that we will bear a "family resemblance." In 1 John 3:2 we are told: "Dear friends, now we are children of God, and what we will be has not yet been made known. But we know that when he appears, we shall be like him, for we shall see him as he is."

There are many benefits in being a child of God, but along with these blessings comes the responsibility of sharing in Christ's sufferings. Those who belong to Christ really cannot expect to be treated better than Christ was. If our lives reflect His to any degree, we will be an uncomfortable reminder of Christ to those who have turned their hearts from Him. Those who are moving toward Christ will move toward us, but those who are moving away from Him will turn away from us. But our motivation in bearing such suffering is that we will one day share in Christ's glory when we come into our full inheritance.

It has been said that God has no natural children on earth, and that is true. All those who have the right to call God "Father" are children by adoption. Like Sean, they have objective proof of this fact. They have the papers to prove their status as sons because the record of their adoption has been preserved forever in the Scriptures. But they also have subjective proof of their right to call God their Father, because each day they have the inner assurance that comes from the Holy Spirit, who testifies with their own spirits that they are the children of God.

Holy Spirit, speak to my heart the reassuring promise that God has accepted me as His own dear

child. Work in my life so that I may reflect the image of
the Christ who has become my brother. Grant me patience each day as I endure adversity for the sake of the
Son, and help me to focus on the glory that is to come.
Amen.

10

GOD'S ELECT

> Who will bring any charge against those
> whom God has chosen? It is God who
> justifies. (*Romans 8:33*)

Two candidates are being interviewed for the same position. Their educations and work histories are similar. They possess comparable skills and both want the job badly. After carefully considering both of them, the employer chooses one and thanks the other for applying. Is the employer being fair? That probably depends upon which candidate you ask. The one who has been chosen for the position will likely applaud the employer for selecting wisely. Suppose, however, that the one who was chosen had absolutely nothing to recommend him or her for the position? What if that person had no experience and no education? Suppose that individual had performed terribly during the interview and had not even dressed appropriately for it? Obviously, the other candidate would feel cheated.

That is how many people respond when they hear the theological term *election,* which literally means "to choose."

It is not the fact that the New Testament often refers to the church as "the elect" or "the chosen" that is so troubling. Rather, it is the basis that God used for making such a choice that poses the problem. According to 1 Peter 1:2, it was a choice based upon the foreknowledge of God. Moreover, Ephesians 1:4 tells us that it was a choice made by God "before the creation of the world."

If we were to trace the beginning of our salvation back to the point when we first exercised faith in Jesus Christ, we haven't gone back far enough. We can go back to the point when we first heard the gospel, and we still aren't there yet. We can even go all the way back to the moment when Jesus Christ died on the cross, but we must still go further. If we are "chosen," then we must go all the way back to the Father's decision to save in order to see where our salvation first took place.

To many people, this seems patently unfair. "If the choice was made before I was born," they say, "made even before the very world in which I now live was created, how can it be fair?" The answer is that it isn't fair. That's because God's choice to save was not based upon fairness but upon the principle of grace. Romans 8:33 says that it is God who chooses and God who justifies. God's choice was based solely upon grace.

In a society that values pragmatism like ours does, such a message is hard to accept. We know that we must work for what we get, and we look up to the person who has made his or her own way in life. Whether or not we like to admit it outwardly, we secretly believe that everyone gets pretty much what they deserve. So when we read that we have been chosen by God, we naturally conclude that somewhere along the way we must have done something to deserve being chosen. But since God's choice is based upon grace, it cannot be rooted in any action or merit of our own.

Those who say that divine election isn't fair are correct. None of us deserves to be in Christ. It is a gift of grace. As a Christian, I had always accepted this as a point of faith, but I don't think that I truly understood it until I watched Martha die of cancer. Over a matter of weeks, she grew thinner and thinner, eventually taking on that pinched, skeletal appearance of someone who has been the victim of starvation. Yet each day that her body weakened, her faith seemed to grow proportionally stronger. Frankly, Martha's confidence bothered me. I didn't see her as someone who "deserved" to have that kind of assurance. As far as I was concerned, she wasn't a very good Christian. She didn't go to church as often as I thought she should. She wasn't involved in any of its ministries. I was fairly sure that she wasn't reading her Bible as much as she should have been. After one of my visits to her in the hospital, I complained to God. "She doesn't deserve to have that kind of peace," I grumbled. "Exactly," came back God's unspoken reply. "Isn't that what grace is all about?" Whatever Martha's weaknesses may have been, she had staked her life on the truth that Jesus Christ had died for her. She wasn't counting on her own righteousness, but on Christ's. So when the time to die finally came, this "average" Christian was able to face it without fear.

The fact that God is the source of our salvation is the basis for our assurance of salvation: "What, then, shall we say in response to this? If God is for us, who can be against us? He who did not spare his own Son, but gave him up for us all—how will

he not also, along with him, graciously give us all
things?" (Romans 8:31–32).

God will not bring a charge against us. On the
contrary, it is He who chose us in grace before the
foundation of the world. Christ will not condemn
us; He is the One who died and rose again to pay
for our sins and now stands at the Father's right
hand and pleads on our behalf.

But why me? Why did God choose to make me
an object of His grace? While not all my questions
in this area can be easily resolved, the Scriptures in-
form me of the motive behind God's choice. It was
based upon love. The employer may make a choice
based upon merit or personal connections, but
God's choice is grounded on His undying love.

*Sovereign God, thank You that You loved me even
before the foundation of the world. I may not have all
the answers to my questions, but I do know that You
chose me in grace and sent Your Son to be my Savior.
Amen.*

11

MY PEOPLE

> As he says in Hosea: "I will call them 'my
> people' who are not my people; and I will
> call her 'my loved one' who is not my loved
> one," and, "It will happen that in the very
> place where it was said to them, 'You are not
> my people,' they will be called 'sons of the
> living God.'" *(Romans 9:25–26)*

In May of 1954, the United States Supreme Court
issued the following decision: "We conclude that
in the field of public education the doctrine of 'separate but equal' has no place. Separate educational
facilities are inherently unequal."

While not immediately accepted by all, this
watershed decision concerning public education
eventually changed many other aspects of American society. Up until this time, certain institutions
were open only to the people of one race, with others excluded on the basis of their skin color. Once
access to schools had been mandated by the federal
government, many other doors eventually opened
as a result.

Gentile worshipers of Israel's God shared a similar experience. Although they were allowed to
worship as proselytes and to offer sacrifices, their
access to the place of worship was limited. They
were permitted to enter the outermost court of the
temple, known as the court of the Gentiles, but
they could not pass beyond it. This area was sepa-

rated from the temple's inner courts by a stone
balustrade, or railing, of several feet in height.
Warnings were posted along this barrier in Greek
and Latin telling Gentiles that they would be put to
death if they went beyond it.

Despite this barrier, the Bible gives evidence of
God's deep and lasting concern for the Gentile nations. When God made a covenant with Abraham,
He promised that Abraham's seed would bless *all*
the nations of the earth (Genesis 22:18). Isaiah later
prophesied that Jesus would be a "light to the Gentiles" (Isaiah 42:6; cf. Luke 2:32). It is this promise
—that God would one day call the Gentiles to Himself—that Paul refers in Romans 9, where he
appeals for scriptural support from two passages in
the book of Hosea.

The prophet Hosea was a kind of living object
lesson to the nation of Israel. He was commanded by
God to marry an adulterous woman, and his children were given names that symbolized God's anger
over Israel's unfaithfulness. The first child was
named Lo-Ruhamah, which literally meant "not-
loved." The second child was called Lo-Ammi, a
name that meant "not my people." Because the
northern tribes had refused to listen to the appeals
of God's prophets to repent, they were to be treated
by God like those who have been divorced or disin-
herited. However, this rejection was only temporary.
Hosea 1:10 promised: "Yet the Israelites will be like
the sand on the seashore, which cannot be mea-
sured or counted. In the place where it was said to
them, 'You are not my people,' they will be called
'sons of the Living God.'" This promise was repeated in Hosea 2:23: "I will plant her for myself in the

land; I will show my love to the one I called 'Not my loved one.' I will say to those called 'Not my people,' 'You are my people'; and they will say, 'You are my God.'"

According to the apostle Paul, these promises were proof of God's willingness to reach out to those who are alienated from Him. Paul was calling the Gentiles to become part of the church. Their acceptance by God, in turn, would spur Israel to recognize Jesus as the Messiah.

Like the people mentioned in these verses, we were alienated from God prior to trusting in Christ for our salvation. Like Israel, our sins had made us God's enemies. The living God was our Creator but not our God. We were His creation but not His people. Like those who were kept from the inner courts of the temple by the wall that separated them from the rest of God's people, we had no direct access into God's presence.

Prior to our trusting in Christ, God could not claim us as His own. Despite our best intentions, we were separated from Him by a wall of sin. It is true that God loved us even then, but because our sin deserved His wrath, God could not freely express that love without compromising His righteous standard. But now that we are in Christ, our status has changed. Jesus has broken down the wall of unfulfilled commandments that kept us from God's presence by fulfilling the law of God on our behalf (Ephesians 2:14–15). He resolved the dilemma posed by our sin by becoming a sin offering for us.

It is easy to forget that we were once strangers to God's promises. In time, we may even come to think that this freedom of access into God's presence is something that was owed to us. Or we may have the opposite problem: We may be so overwhelmed by the mistakes in our past that we cannot possibly see how God could accept us. These verses provide a remedy for both extremes. For the complacent, they offer a reminder that there was once a time when we had no legitimate right to call on the God we now worship. We did not deserve God's love but only His anger. Every opportunity to pray, worship, and serve God is a gift. For those troubled by their past sins, these verses offer the encouragement of knowing that God is pleased to reach out to those who are alienated from Him. Whatever our past, if we come to Him in Christ, God will accept us.

These words also provide us with an example of the kind of attitude that we are to have toward others. Just as God was willing to reach out to those who had distanced themselves from Him, we have a responsibility to reach out to others. Like Hosea's wife and children, they will often seem like unlikely candidates for our interest. But our God seeks the unlovable and the uninterested. He is a God who reaches out to people just like us!

My God and Savior, thank You for opening the way into Your presence through Your Son Jesus. Open my eyes to see others as You see them and to seek those that You are seeking. Amen.

12

THOSE WHO CALL UPON THE NAME OF THE LORD JESUS CHRIST

> To the church of God in Corinth, to those sanctified in Christ Jesus and called to be holy, together with all those everywhere who call on the name of our Lord Jesus Christ— their Lord and ours. *(1 Corinthians 1:2)*

Corinth must have seemed an unlikely location for a church. It is true that it was a major trading port and, in many ways, the gateway to the world. But Corinth was also a popular center for pagan worship, and the city was so well known for immorality that elsewhere it was considered an insult to call someone a Corinthian. One of the city's most famous tourist attractions was the temple of Aphrodite, which was served by a thousand religious prostitutes. These cult prostitutes performed acts of sexual immorality with those who came to the temple to worship.

But despite these conditions, a lively church developed in Corinth. However, it was a church with problems that reflected its surroundings. Some of its members continued to frequent the pagan temples and join in their feasts. Others practiced sexual immorality of all kinds, including one notorious case that was so tolerated by the church's members that they actually boasted about it to others (1 Corinthians 5:2). This "free spirit" mentality also affected the Corinthians' worship and threatened to turn services into chaos.

In view of this, it is somewhat surprising to hear Paul use the language of holiness to describe the Corinthian Christians. He referred to them as those who had been "sanctified in Christ Jesus" and notes that they were "called to be holy." More precisely, he uses the term "holy ones" or "saints" to refer to them.

Throughout church history, it hasn't been uncommon for people to speak in glowing terms of the saints, even when it wasn't deserved. For example, the grave of a popular Welsh saint was being excavated during the renovation of the chapel dedicated in his honor, but the unearthed skeleton proved to be that of a pregnant woman. When an anthropologist pointed this out to the monk in charge of the project, he seemed unbothered by it. "The saint was a very remarkable man," he explained.

For centuries, Christian tradition has portrayed the saints as superhuman beings. But this is certainly not the impression we get of the believers at Corinth. If this was a church full of saints, it was a church very much like our own. The Corinthians were troubled by theological controversy and split by divided loyalties. While many of its members were tremendously gifted, they were also very ordinary. There were no gaunt-cheeked saints sporting halos in this crowd!

The two terms Paul used to characterize the Corinthian believers are related. The term *sanctify* is really a verbal form of the word *holy*. This is also true of the English term, which comes from *sanctus*, the Latin word for holy. Throughout the Bible, when something was sanctified, it was set apart for special use. That which is set apart for God's use becomes "holy." For example, the seventh day of the week was "sanctified," in the sense that it was set apart by God as being distinct from the other days of the week (Genesis 2:3). And the firstborn of Israel were set apart for God's use (Exodus 13:2).

It is our relationship with Jesus that sets us apart as Christians. The Bible says that we are sanctified when we "call upon the name" of Jesus Christ. This is true in several respects. We call upon Him for salvation (Acts 2:21; 9:14). We have been baptized in the name of Christ (1 Corinthians 1:13). When we pray, we make our requests in the authority of His name (John 15:16). In fact, there is a sense in which every action of the believer is done in the name of Christ: "And whatever you do, whether in word or deed, do it all in the name of the Lord Jesus, giving thanks to God the Father through him" (Colossians 3:17).

But calling on the name of Jesus is not a form of word magic. It does not mean that something supernatural happens whenever the Christian speaks the name of Jesus. The seven sons of the Jewish chief priest Sceva made this mistake when they attempted to use Jesus' name as a charm for casting out demons. They had seen the apostle Paul exercise authority over the demonic powers in Jesus' name and attempted to imitate him. They invoked His name by saying, "In the name of Jesus, whom Paul preaches, I command you to come out." The results were disastrous. Instead of leaving the victim, the evil spirit answered them, saying, "Jesus I know and I know about Paul, but who are you?" The next thing that the sons of Sceva knew, the de-

mon-possessed man had overpowered all seven of
them and given them such a beating that they fled
from the scene naked and bleeding (Acts
19:13–16).

When we call upon the name of the Lord, we
recognize Christ's work. Those who call upon the
name of Jesus do so because: "Salvation is found in
no one else, for there is no other name under heav-
en given to men by which we must be saved" (Acts
4:12). We also recognize Christ's authority when
we call upon His name. The New Testament term
for "Lord" is "*Kurios*," which implies authority to
rule. So to say that Jesus is Lord recognizes His
right to govern our lives. But even more important-
ly, when we call upon the name of the Lord, we
recognize Christ's deity. In the Greek translation of
the Old Testament, the term *Kurios* is used most often as a title for God. Those who say that Jesus is
Lord recognize that He is God incarnate. He is worthy of worship.

We may be surprised to hear Paul describe the
Corinthians as "saints," but they are not unique.
Whether in a city like Corinth, known for its
wickedness, or in a small town whose horizon is
spotted with steeples, all those who call upon the
name of Jesus Christ as Lord are saints.

*Lord Jesus, I recognize Your power to save and
Your authority over my life. I offer You my worship,
along with all the other saints who call upon Your
name. Amen.*

13

THE SAVED

> For the message of the cross is foolishness to those who are perishing, but to us who are being saved it is the power of God. *(1 Corinthians 1:18)*

The rescue mission, located on one of the city's most rundown avenues, is surrounded by dingy bars and crumbling buildings. It looks like a concrete bunker. In fact, its gray features are so nondescript that it would be difficult to tell what kind of building it was—if it weren't for the large cross that juts out from its side. At night, the outline of the cross glows in red neon, blinking out the message emblazoned at its center: "Jesus Saves." In a way, this rescue mission, along with those who stumble into it for help, provides a living example of Paul's message in 1 Corinthians 1:18. Its sputtering neon sign underscores the theme of this verse: Jesus saves by the power of the Cross.

Because of their tradition of philosophic inquiry and a long history of great orators, the Corinthians had difficulty accepting this message. To them, its most embarrassing feature was its emphasis upon the cross, an instrument used to execute criminals, slaves, and those who were traitors to the state. Roman citizens were exempt from this form of punishment. Those who died on the cross were stripped naked and subjected to public humiliation. The very fact that they suffered in such a way was itself testimony of the shame and power-lessness of those who were crucified. Yet Paul's message maintained that in Jesus' case the cross was actually a display of divine power. To Corinthi-an understanding, this seemed like nonsense.

Moreover, Paul's style of delivery did not seem eloquent enough for the Corinthians, especially when compared with some of the other speakers who had visited the church (1 Corinthians 1:12; 2 Corinthians 10:10). To the Greek mind, the man-ner of delivery was almost as important as the message itself. This expectation of eloquence had been shaped by many who had followed in the tra-dition of the famous Greek orators like Demosthenes (384–322 B.C.), who was said to have locked him-self away in his study for weeks at a time practicing his speeches, and who cured himself of a stammer by speaking with pebbles in his mouth. He also re-cited poetry while running uphill, in order to develop greater breath control.

But the apostle Paul seemed to deliberately shy away from these finer points of rhetorical tech-nique: "When I came to you, brothers, I did not come with eloquence or superior wisdom as I pro-claimed to you the testimony about God. For I re-solved to know nothing while I was with you except Jesus Christ and him crucified" (1 Corinthians 2:1–2).

Ultimately, however, it was not Paul's style that kept others from seeing the value of his message, but their spiritual state. Paul's message seemed fool-ish to those who lacked the insight given by the Holy Spirit to those who are in Christ. They were spiritually dead and therefore spiritually blind. It was a diagnosis of their standing before God. It is, in fact, a diagnosis of all of humankind's standing before God since sin first entered the picture.

When Adam was placed by God in the Garden of Eden to tend it, he was told that it was permissible to eat of all the trees in the garden except one. He was not to eat of the tree of the knowledge of good and evil: ". . . for when you eat of it you will surely die" (Genesis 2:17). Unfortunately, Adam did eat of the tree and he did die. His physical death wasn't until several hundred years later, but, spiritually speaking, the effect of his disobedience was immediate. As soon as he disobeyed God, Adam was overtaken with a sense of shame and alienation. He hid from God and tried to shift the blame for his actions to his wife, Eve (Genesis 3:7–12).

This is what Paul means when he says that his message seems like foolishness to those who are perishing. Because they are alienated from God by sin, those who are perishing cannot appreciate the value of Christ or His work. They are in the throes of spiritual death, of which physical death is only a symptom.

On the other hand, Paul says that those who accept the message of the cross are being saved. It is significant that Paul uses the present tense for both cases. Those who reject the message of Christ *are* perishing. Those who accept the message are being saved.

When the New Testament speaks of the believer's salvation, it does so in three tenses: past, present, and future. We have been saved, we are being saved, and we will be saved.

The New Testament speaks of salvation in the
past tense and says that the salvation of those who
have trusted in Jesus Christ is an accomplished fact
(Romans 8:24; 2 Timothy 1:9). Jesus has completed the sacrifice for sin that God required, and
nothing can be added to or subtracted from what
He has done. In this respect, those who are now in
Christ are as saved as they will ever be.

But at the same time, Paul uses the present
tense when he speaks of salvation in 1 Corinthians
1:18, where he speaks of salvation as something
that the believer is currently undergoing. Because
Christ's work also leads to a gradual transformation
in the believer's life, one that is brought about by
the Holy Spirit, it can legitimately be said that we
are in the process of *being* saved. Those who are being saved know the power of the cross on a
personal level. For them, the cross is more than a
symbol of an historical event that they look back
upon with gratitude. For them, it has daily impact
(Galatians 2:20).

There is also a future dimension to salvation.
The work of Christ on the cross has been completed, but the believer's experience of redemption has
not. We *have been* saved, we *are being* saved, and we
will be saved. We will be saved from God's wrath
through Christ (Romans 5:9), and our personal salvation will be completed when we are resurrected
(1 Corinthians 15:52–54).

The statement that "Jesus saves" is so familiar
to those who know Christ that it has almost become a cliché. We say it and sing it without
thinking much about its implications. It sounds so
old-fashioned that we may even feel a bit embar-

rassed when we pass by the rescue mission and see its bright message beaming in the dark. But we should not, for it summarizes our hope and defines who we are in Christ. We are the saved. We are those who have been saved and are resting on the finished work of Christ. We are those who are now being saved and daily walk in the transforming power of the living God. And we are those who look forward to being saved, with the confidence that the shed blood of Jesus will shield us from the wrath to come.

Heavenly Father, never let me fail to see the glory of the simple truth that Jesus saves. Use me to share this message with others. Open the minds and hearts of those who hear it. Amen.

14
GOD'S FELLOW WORKERS

> For we are God's fellow workers; you are
> God's field, God's building. (*1 Corinthians
> 3:9*)

On a sunny Saturday morning as I walked along behind the lawn mower, my seven-year-old son Jarred squeezed in front of front of me and grasped the mower's handle. Because he was so small, he did not have enough strength to steer the mower, so I pushed it for him. I had to walk much slower than normal to match his small strides. Consequently, the job took about twice as long as usual to finish. When we were done, Jarred rushed into the house, beamed up at his mother and said: "I helped Daddy cut the grass!"

It is easy to see ourselves in this picture when we read that we are "God's fellow workers." Just as Jarred didn't actually steer the lawn mower, we do not "steer" the affairs of the church but follow God's lead by paying attention to the directives He has provided for us in Scripture. We do not move the work of God forward by our own power, but must rely upon the empowerment and gifts of the Holy Spirit.

It is easy to think that our imperfect attempts to help God actually slow the work rather than speed it to its completion. This is true in many respects. The affairs of the church have been ordered by the Lord. One of the purposes of God's Word is to tell us "how people ought to conduct themselves in God's household" (1 Timothy 3:15). Our opinions and personal taste have no place in those areas where God has given definitive direction.

At the same time, God has given certain believers the responsibility of exercising leadership in the church (Hebrews 13:17). The elders of the church have been commanded to "shepherd the flock of God" (1 Peter 5:2). The shepherd goes before the flock and provides the needed direction for those who follow.

It is also true that we are dependent upon God's power to fulfill the tasks He has called us to perform as His fellow workers. The apostle Paul ascribed his own success to this fact, yet in the same breath readily admitted that he had worked harder than any of his contemporaries: "But by the grace of God I am what I am, and his grace to me was not without effect. No, I worked harder than all of them—yet not I, but the grace of God that was with me" (1 Corinthians 15:10).

Paul's claim in this verse raises a very important question: Is God sovereign in all that the church accomplishes, or do we play a determinative role in whether or not the church will be effective in its mission? God's Word affirms that both are true. Nowhere is this seen more clearly than in the promise of Christ's second coming. On the one hand, Jesus said that this day has been fixed by God, that He alone knows the day and the time (Matthew 24:36; Mark 13:32). But despite this, believers ". . . look forward to the day of God and

speed its coming" (2 Peter 3:12). Empowered by
the Holy Spirit, our efforts make a real contribution
to the accomplishment of God's ultimate purposes.
So in some mysterious way, we can actually hasten
the time of Christ's arrival without interfering with
His sovereignty.

The reality of human responsibility is evident
in another way. We are told in the Scriptures that
our efforts as God's fellow workers will be evaluated
and rewarded. The apostle Paul carried out the
tasks assigned to him by God like an expert builder,
but he warned others to be careful about how they
built upon the foundation he had laid. He also
warned that the rewards received by those who
serve God will be commensurate with the quality of
the workmanship (1 Corinthians 3:10–15).

While we are God's fellow workers, we are also
fellow workers with one another. Our gifts, abilities, and individual tasks differ. Nevertheless, they
all contribute to the same purpose. We are not
building our own individual kingdom. Our efforts
are dedicated to Christ and His kingdom.

Several years ago, I met a man named Charlie
who told me of the time when he felt God urging
him to visit a nearby pastor. "As I lay there drunk,"
he explained, "God spoke to me and told me to get
up and call the pastor and get saved." He went to
see the pastor at his office, and during the visit the
pastor prayed with Charlie to receive Christ. From
that moment on, a number of changes began to
take place in Charlie's life. He was one of the very
few to be accepted at a unique private college in
New York, where he was trained to be a civil engineer. One of the achievements he was most proud

of was that he had worked on the Empire State Building. "Every time I went past it," he said with a grin, "I would think to myself, 'I had a part in raising that up.'"

Those of us who know Christ are part of a much bigger project. Every believer has a role to play in the construction of the church of Jesus Christ. We do not all have the same function, nor do we all have the same degree of visibility. Nevertheless, we all are necessary, and each of us will be asked to give account of our work. Will we be ashamed on that day to realize that we have squandered our God-given gifts and abilities on trivialities? Or will we see all our weariness, pain, and struggle disappear as we hear Him say, "Well done, my good and faithful servant"?

Heavenly Father, thank You for making me one of Your coworkers. Help me to labor skillfully with the strength and skill that Your Spirit provides. I look forward to the day when my work is tested and approved and I hear You say, "Well done!" Amen.

15
GOD'S FIELD

For we are God's fellow workers; you are
God's field, God's building. (*1 Corinthians
3:9*)

I used to think that farming was easy. It had to be.
All the farmer had to do is put the seed in the
ground, wait for it to rain, reap the harvest, and
collect the profit. How difficult could that be? Very
difficult, as I learned when I became the pastor of a
church in a farming community.

Although planting seems simple, it requires so-
phisticated equipment costing hundreds of
thousands of dollars to ensure that the seed is
planted in the right location and at the right depth.
And even before the seed can be planted, the field
needs to be prepared. The ground must be turned
and fertilized. Once the seed is sown, the young
plants must be cultivated. And while the farmer
cannot control the rain, it is possible to give the
rain a helping hand with irrigation equipment. After the harvest, selling the crop often requires a
knowledge of the international markets. I learned
very quickly living in that community that farming
was much more difficult than it looked. The farmers
I knew needed the skill of a chemist, the mechani-
cal know-how of an engineer, the financial ability
of a Wall Street lawyer, and the patience of Job!

God is a farmer. According to 1 Corinthians 3:9, we are "God's field." Like the fields of the farmers in my congregation, God's field needs to be sown, watered, cultivated, and harvested. God, however, uses people instead of machines to do His work. In the case of the Corinthian church, He used people like Paul and Apollos: "I planted the seed, Apollos watered it, but God made it grow" (1 Corinthians 3:6).

The Corinthians enjoyed a distinguished succession of ministers unparalleled by any other church in history. Unfortunately, instead of benefiting from this, they began to divide themselves into various camps as a result. Some identified with Apollos and said that his ministry was more important than that of Paul. Others favored one of the other famous teachers who had visited Corinth. And one group refused to acknowledge the value of any human teacher at all, and identified themselves only as followers of Jesus.

This scriptural account is a warning to us that good preaching, as important as it is, does not always guarantee spiritual growth. The church of Corinth was exposed to the best preaching the New Testament era had to offer, yet it only seemed to divide the congregation. Paul responded to this "fan club" mentality by reminding the people that God alone is responsible for growth: "So neither he who plants nor he who waters is anything, but only God who makes things grow" (1 Corinthians 3:7). In other words, those who do the preaching are merely the instruments God used to accomplish His purpose.

The farmer uses a tractor for one purpose and a

combine for another. His decision to use one over
another is based upon the immediate need of the
field. The same is true of God's field. The church
does not always need the fiery preaching of an
Apollos. At times, it is better served by the steady
teaching of a Paul or the practical application of a
Simon Peter.

The farmer's choice of seed is determined by
the type of crop that is desired. Different kinds of
seeds produce different kinds of crops. God, on the
other hand, has only one kind of seed: His Word.
Where God is concerned, however, the same seed
can accomplish several purposes. In some circumstances, God uses His Word to give new life. Those
who are saved are born again by the incorruptible
seed of the Word of God (1 Peter 1:23). God also
uses the Word to water what has already been
planted (Isaiah 55:10–11). Paul planted and Apollos watered, but they both used God's Word.

While God promises in Isaiah 55:10–11 that
His word will always accomplish the purpose He
intended, Jesus warned that not everyone who
hears the word will benefit from it (Matthew
13:1–9; Mark 4:1–9; Luke 8:4–8). In the parable of
the sower, Jesus described four instances in which
the seed of the Word was sown with distinctly different results. The difference in each case was not
due to the seed but to the soil.

Jesus tells us that there are times when the
Word of God seems to have no effect at all on those
who hear it. When this happens, two factors are at
work. According to Jesus, the Word fails to produce
results when those who hear do not understand. Jesus also warned that Satan is actively involved in

"stealing" the Word (Matthew 13:19; Mark 4:15; Luke 8:12). At other times, the seed seems to produce remarkable results at first, but the fruit quickly withers away. The problem in this case is that the response of those who hear is merely superficial, and the seed never truly takes root. So when obedience to the Word brings problems or persecution, they quickly turn away from it (Matthew 13:21; Mark 4:17; Luke 8:13).

In the third scenario described by Jesus, the initial results also seem promising, but the seed is soon choked out by "weeds." In this case, there is too much competition for the Word of God. Its effect is neutralized by the "worries of this life and the deceitfulness of wealth" (Matthew 13:22; Mark 4:19; Luke 8:14).

Jesus said that it is only the "good soil" that produces a harvest. Interestingly, even here the results may vary. In some, the seed produces a hundredfold return. But in others, it is sixty, and in others, thirty (Matthew 13:23; Mark 4:20). The critical factor for those Jesus characterizes as "good soil" is the attitude of the heart (Luke 8:15).

How can we ensure that we will be the kind of field that will bear fruit for God? Fortunately, the solution lies with God Himself. If our problem is one of understanding, we need to ask God for wisdom. If it is a matter of persecution, we need to expect opposition and ask God for the strength to persevere. If the problem is distraction by the cares of this life, we need to broaden our perspective and think in terms of eternity. We need to ask God to show us what the things that seem so important now will mean to us in a million years. Many of them will pass into oblivion, but God's Word stands forever.

Living Word, open my eyes to see the truth of Scripture. Open my heart to respond in faith and obedience. Do not allow Satan to steal the Word but grant me the patience to bear with the trials that come with obedience. Give me an eternal perspective in all that I do. Amen.

16

GOD'S BUILDING

For we are God's fellow workers; you are God's field, God's building. (*1 Corinthians 3:9*)

I think it's great!" David beamed.

"You think it's great that no one is willing to volunteer to work in the nursery?" I asked in amazement.

"That's right," David explained. "I think it's great because it means that everyone would rather be edified."

Most of us would tend to agree with David, and with good reason. Edification is important in the Christian life. God has designed the church so that its members build one another up in the faith (Ephesians 4:12). In the Bible, the word *edify* means "to build up or restore." It is related to the third metaphor used by Paul to describe the church in this verse. He says, "You are . . . God's building." The apostle saw himself as one of those given the task of building a house for God. In the Greek translation of the Old Testament, known as the Septuagint, the verbal form of this word is used to speak of God's effort to build up His people, Israel (Jeremiah 24:6). In the New Testament, it refers to the process of building up the church.

Those who work on God's building edify the

church. As a result of their ministry, God's people are strengthened and more firmly established in their spiritual lives. When you have been edified, you have been spiritually nourished.

In the natural realm, we strive for a balance between nourishment and exercise. To emphasize one element and exclude the other is clearly detrimental to our physical bodies. Some time ago, I visited a doctor because I was suffering from symptoms of exhaustion and depression. After a thorough examination, the doctor asked me two simple questions: "Are you eating regularly?" and "Are you getting enough exercise?" With a few basic changes in my lifestyle, the problem was easily solved.

We also need to seek that kind of balance in the spiritual realm. The temptation we face in the spiritual realm is the danger of becoming addicted to edification. Of course, as God's house, we need to be built up. But the ministry of edification is also meant to equip us to serve others. The goal of edification, according to Ephesians 4:12, is "to prepare God's people for works of service." What is most striking about the concept of edification in the New Testament is that it invariably focuses upon our obligation to edify someone else.

This means that when we come together as a congregation, it is both to be edified and to edify. In this respect, God's building is unlike any other that we have seen, because it actually builds itself. This work of edification is an obligation shared by every believer: "Each of us should please his neighbor for his good, to build him up" (Romans 15:2). We are not to look out for our own personal interests exclusively, but we are also to focus on the interests of others (Philippians 2:3–4).

This principle is especially important when applied to the problem of sin in the believer's life. Spiritual decline, on both an individual and congregational level, proceeds along terrifyingly ordinary terrain. The spiritual degenerate does not suddenly undergo a metamorphosis that leaves him an idolater or sexual pervert. This condition is arrived at by way of more mundane acts of disobedience, such as greed, malice, envy, and rebellion (Romans 1:29–30).

We tend to regard spiritual growth as a purely private matter. However, spiritual life also has a corporate dimension. The apostle Paul compared the effect of sin to that of yeast, implying that the sin of one person can have an impact on many others (1 Corinthians 5:6).

If my spiritual state has the potential to affect yours, mutual accountability is important. However, if you have the capacity to restore me to health, it is essential. The beauty of God's building is that, like the human body, it has the capacity to repair itself. Our accountability is not only to one another, but also to God. He evaluates both the kind of materials that we use and the quality of our workmanship in building His house: "By the grace God has given me, I laid a foundation as an expert builder, and someone else is building on it. But each one should be careful how he builds" (1 Corinthians 3:10).

One summer, a storm that roared through our community damaged the roof of our house. As soon as the men came to repair it, my wife, Jane, stopped what she was doing to watch. She sat in a

folding chair in our driveway and looked on while
they worked. When the foreman saw her, he nervously asked, "You're not going to sit there and
watch are you?" "Of course I am," she replied. "It's
my roof and I want to make sure that you do it right!"

In the same way, God carefully scrutinizes our
efforts to build His house. We might be daunted by
such an audience, if it weren't for the fact that the
same God who evaluates our work has also
equipped us for the task. The expectations that
those who work on God's house use only the best
materials is not unreasonable. Those who build are
empowered by God's Spirit and draw from His un-
limited resources.

In the Old Testament, God equipped individuals to build for Him. During the construction of the
Tabernacle, God chose Bezalel and Oholiab and
filled them with the Spirit in a way that gave them
unique abilities to work with gold, silver, and
bronze. These two men did not work alone, however. They were supported by a team of divinely
skilled craftsmen to make the tent and all its furnishings (Exodus 31:1–11). When Solomon built
the temple in Jerusalem, God sent him Huram-Abi
of Tyre, a man skilled in working with bronze
(2 Chronicles 2:13–14). When the wall around Jerusalem was being rebuilt after the exile, God gave
Nehemiah special leadership abilities and provided
many willing workers to complete a task that on the
surface seemed to be hopeless (Nehemiah 3:1–32).

God continues to provide skilled workers to
contribute to His building project, and we are those
workers. Like those God used in the Old Testament, each one of us brings unique skills to the

work. Because every believer possesses the Holy Spirit, every believer has a contribution to make.

Holy Spirit, equip me to edify others as we work together on God's house. Amen.

17

GOD'S TEMPLE

> Don't you know that you yourselves are
> God's temple and that God's Spirit lives in
> you? *(1 Corinthians 3:16)*

Drive through any large city today and you will see the walls of many buildings covered with graffiti. It may only be a name and date, or it may be something more sinister, such as gang signs or obscenities. An entire wall may even be covered with a spray-painted mural. One of the justifications of those who engage in this practice is that it is actually an art form. Those who consider graffiti painting to be a form of vandalism, however, are quick to point out that the problem with this so called "art form" is that it uses other people's property as its canvas.

While you and I might accidentally damage someone else's property, we would never think of entering that person's home to intentionally deface or destroy it. In fact, if our neighbors were to ask us to watch their home while they went away on vacation, we would be especially vigilant to make sure no one damaged it.

In 1 Corinthians 3:16 we are told to exercise similar care over God's property. In particular, the apostle Paul reminds us that we are God's temple.

The Corinthians were very familiar with the

idea of a temple. Their pagan background was filled with them. Therefore, the language used by Paul in this verse would have brought to the Corinthians' minds the many familiar shrines that surrounded them, and in which were placed statues of the Greek and Roman pantheon.

Those who were from a Jewish background, however, would think of something quite different when they read Paul's words. For them, there was only one temple, just as there was only one true God. The reader from a Jewish background would see the word *temple* and immediately think of Jerusalem and the temple of Jehovah. More specifically, the particular word used by Paul in this verse would bring to mind the sanctuary itself—the place where God demonstrated His presence in a visible way through the shekinah cloud. Although the term *Shekinah* does not appear in the Old Testament, it was used by the rabbis to speak of the glorious cloud which went before Israel during the wilderness journey.

When Israel traveled through the wilderness, God made His presence known by means of a cloud that traveled before them by day and a pillar of fire that gave light by night (Exodus 13:21–22). When the tabernacle was completed, the cloud of glory filled it to such a degree that even Moses could not enter it (Exodus 40:34–35). God did the same when the temple of Solomon was dedicated, causing the priests to flee from the sanctuary (1 Kings 8:11). The tabernacle and the temple were both visible reminders that God had chosen to dwell among His people.

Because of this, one of the greatest tragedies in

the history of the Jewish people was the destruction of Solomon's temple by the Babylonians. They saw the decree by Cyrus, king of Persia in 538 B.C., that permitted them to return and rebuild the temple as a singular mark of God's deliverance. However, in an event that was prophesied by Jesus in Luke 21:6, the temple was destroyed again by the Romans in 70 A.D., nearly twenty years after Paul penned these words.

Paul does not say that we are "*a* temple," as if there were many. He says that we are "*the* temple." He is saying that the church is the one true temple of the living God. This description is all the more significant when we realize that the temple in Jerusalem was still functioning at the time Paul wrote these words.

The church is the new temple, a dwelling place for God through the presence of the Holy Spirit. The fact that God has chosen the church to be His temple places us under obligation. Being the temple of God means that we are also accountable as caretakers of it: "If anyone destroys God's temple, God will destroy him; for God's temple is sacred, and you are that temple" (1 Corinthians 3:17).

Although this is the kind of warning we might normally expect to find in the Old Testament, it is also consistent with the New Testament. For example, when Ananias and Sapphira conspired together to lie to the Holy Spirit, they were severely judged. As a result: "Great fear seized the whole church and all who heard about these events" (Acts 5:11). These tragic deaths were a proof of God's ownership of the church and a solemn reminder of the reality of divine judgment.

I once visited a church and noticed that the building was in bad condition. The paint was peeling, the steps were cracked and crumbling, and the sign out front had several letters missing from the church's name. In every aspect, the building made a statement about this church and its members. In bold letters, it said: "We don't care." The way a church takes care of its building and grounds says a lot about it. But the way a church lives says even more. There are signs of neglect that are far more serious than peeling paint and crumbling cement.

Since the church is God's dwelling, we should be concerned about its condition. If there are weaknesses, we should strive to build them up. Where there is failure, we should work toward restoration. We cannot show any less regard for God's house than we would for our own. The blemishes that mar the true temple are things like unkind speech, envy, factions, and outbursts of anger. One couple who grumbled about some of the decisions the new pastor of the church they attended had made justified their anger by saying: "After all, its our church!" They were mistaken. It is not the congregation's church. It is not the board's church or even the pastor's, either. The church belongs to God. It is His temple, and He will hold us accountable if we do anything to harm it.

Lord of the Church, glorify Yourself through Your people. Make me Your instrument to build up the church. May the glory of Your presence shine through Your people so that others will know it is Your dwelling place. Amen.

18

SERVANTS OF CHRIST

So then, men ought to regard us as servants of Christ and as those entrusted with the secret things of God. *(1 Corinthians 4:1)*

The Corinthians' regard for their favorite teachers had so divided the church that its members were identifying themselves as being "of" Paul, Apollos, or Cephas (Peter). Paul countered this mentality by pointing out that those who had preached the Word at Corinth were merely servants of Christ. In so doing, Paul used the language of slavery to refer to his ministry.

In the apostle Paul's day, slaves were regarded as property rather than persons. The slave, whose function was to serve his or her master, could be bought and sold at the discretion of the master and were often subjected to harsh treatment. It has been estimated that nearly one-third of the population of the city of Corinth consisted of slaves. Although they were a critical factor in the economy of the Roman empire, the tasks that slaves performed were considered too menial for those who were free. The Greeks in particular, regarded slaves with contempt.

In the biblical text, the term that is translated "servants" is one that referred to an assistant or a helper. In effect, Paul was telling the Corinthians that they should regard those who had preached the Word to them as Christ's "underlings." The same Greek word is used by Luke, the apostle Paul's frequent traveling companion, in referring to those who first delivered the gospel message as "servants of the word" (Luke 1:2). In light of that, Paul, Apollos, and Cephas were not superstars but merely servants charged with the responsibility of dispensing God's Word.

Paul also uses the word *steward* to refer to this ministry. The steward was literally a household manager, someone who was responsible for the daily administration of the master's affairs.

The steward was often a slave who was put in charge of other slaves and distributed the master's goods to them. The steward's primary obligation was tending to the master's interests (Luke 12:42–43; 1 Corinthians 4:2).

Like the stewards, Paul and his colleagues were given the responsibility of dispensing the "secret things of God," or literally "the mysteries of God." In Greek religion and philosophy, the word *mystery* was used to refer to truths that were revealed only to initiates. Paul had been entrusted with God's revealed truth, and as a steward, he exercised a measure of authority. It was authority derived from God. The truths he proclaimed did not originate with him.

Paul characterized himself more particularly as a steward of God's grace to the Gentiles (Ephesians 3:2; Colossians 1:25–27). While his role was unique in many ways, all Christians share a similar stewardship. We are all stewards of God's manifold grace: "Each one should use whatever gift he has received to serve others, faithfully administering God's grace in its various forms" (1 Peter 4:10). Whether our gifts are intended to be used in the public arena or in the private, we are to derive our strength from God and to the primary goal of bringing Him glory.

Elsewhere, Paul referred to himself using the term *diakonos*, a word that literally means "one who waits on tables" (1 Corinthians 3:5; 2 Corinthians 6:4). It is the same term used of the servants who came to draw water at the wedding feast in Cana (John 2:9). Paul compared his ministry and that of his colleagues to the role of a common household slave who provided table service while the master's family ate.

Paul also used the word *doulos* to refer to himself, even placing it before that of apostle (Romans 1:1). Although most English versions translate this word as "servant," his original readers would have recognized that he was identifying himself as a bond slave in the service of Christ.

Many of the people who read this were themselves slaves in a literal sense. Paul instructed Christian slaves to obey their earthly masters, with the knowledge that such obedience was a form of serving Christ (1 Timothy 6:1; Ephesians 6:6). For some, this radical call to discipleship had grave implications. The apostle Peter urged Christian slaves to show respect, even to those masters who physically mistreated them (1 Peter 2:18–25). The use of the slave metaphor and the call to slaves to obey their masters, however, should not be seen as a biblical endorsement of the practice of slavery. In 1 Corinthians 7:21, Paul told Christian slaves to obtain their freedom by legitimate means whenever possible, and he asked Philemon to free the runaway slave Onesimus (Philemon 16).

From the biblical perspective, then, the Christian has a dual status. Paul reminded Christian slaves that they were free in Christ, and he reminded the free that they were slaves of Christ (1 Corinthians 7:22). Like Paul, all Christians are servants of God.

This call to be Christ's servants is absolute. It demands complete surrender, even to the point of death: "Whoever serves me must follow me; and where I am, my servant also will be. My Father will honor the one who serves me" (John 12:26). Christ Himself has set the standard for us, showing His followers what the servant's lifestyle is like. By becoming incarnate, the Lord took on the form of a bond servant (Philippians 2:7). He performed the task of a household slave when He washed the disciples' feet and urged them to follow His example: "You call me 'Teacher' and 'Lord,' and rightly so, for that is what I am. Now that I, your Lord and Teacher, have washed your feet, you also should wash one another's feet" (John 13:13–14).

The title of servant is a needed corrective for a church living in an age that is obsessed with individual freedom and personal choice. Because we are servants of Christ, we do not live to please ourselves. We live only to please Him, our Lord and Master.

Lord Jesus, thank You for the stewardship of grace You have entrusted to me. Show me in this day how I can be faithful to that calling. Amen.

19

THOSE ON WHOM THE FULFILLMENT
OF THE AGES HAS COME

> These things happened to them as ex-
> amples and were written down as warnings
> for us, on whom the fulfillment of the ages
> has come. (1 Corinthians 10:11)

Time is important to me. It is so important, in
fact, that I "wear" time on my wrist in the form
of a watch. I want to know what time it is, even
when I don't have anywhere to go. Down through
the ages, humanity has devised countless ways of
marking the passage of the hours—from sun dials
to water clocks to digital wristwatches. Our interest
in time is understandable, since it is a nonrenew-
able commodity.

God is also interested in time. This is not because He is subject to its limitations, as we are, but
because time is the vehicle He uses to unfold His
eternal purposes. God is not time-bound, but He is
time-conscious. The Bible says that Christ's death
took place "at just the right time" (Romans 5:6,
NIV). This sense of divine purpose is also reflected
in 1 Corinthians 10:11, where Paul describes believers as those "on whom the fulfillment of the
ages have come." Similar language is used in Hebrews 1:2, which says that although God has
spoken in many times and ways in the past, He has
spoken through His Son in "these last days."

Jesus spoke of the "present age" and "the age to

come." The present age was the time in which He and His disciples were currently living. According to Jesus, the age to come will be signaled by His second coming and the judgment of the wicked (Matthew 13:49; 24:3). It will also be the time when God's people inherit their eternal life (Mark 10:30).

Jesus also taught that certain cataclysmic events would take place at the close of the present age. He said that famines, earthquakes, and a growing hardness of heart will prepare the way for the "abomination that causes desolation," or Antichrist. The appearance of Antichrist, in turn, will usher in a period of unequaled distress, or the Tribulation. At the close of this time, a sign will appear in the heavens, and Jesus will return with power and glory (Matthew 24:4–31). And when Jesus Christ returns, He will not be alone. He will bring with Him those who have trusted in Him (1 Thessalonians 3:13).

It is this great event to which everything that has occurred in this present age has been building. That is why Paul describes the age in which we are currently living as the "fulfillment of the ages." In ancient Greek, this term referred to a point of culmination or a goal.

This does not mean, however, that Paul was so focused on the future that he had no interest in the present. Nor does it mean that he felt that the past was unimportant. We are told just the opposite in 1 Corinthians 10:11. This verse tells us that our approach to the present should be shaped by our expectation that Christ will return soon, and that we should also be aware of the lessons that can be learned from the past.

The importance of the present is reflected in

the fact that God wants us to apply biblical principles to our current circumstances. His concern is
not merely for the "by and by." He is deeply interested in the way we live in the "here and now."

The importance of the past is demonstrated in
the fact that many of the principles that help us in
the present come from the Old Testament. That is
what it means in 1 Corinthians 10:11, where it
says, "These things . . . were written down as warnings for us." These scriptural truths will be
especially helpful in preparing us to face temptation (1 Corinthians 10:12–13). The fate of those
who ignored God's commands will provide a
solemn reminder of the consequences of disobedience. But the example of those who obeyed in the
face of great difficulty will give us confidence
whenever we find ourselves similarly tempted.
Their stories will provide objective proof that God
will never allow us to be tempted without providing a way out (1 Corinthians 10:13).

Because God is not subject to time limitations
like we are, His sense of "timing" is quite different
from ours. What seems to us like an interminable
delay is no delay at all to Him. The apostle Peter
warned that some would misinterpret the time
lapse between the end of this age and beginning of
the next, noting that what some would take to be
"slowness" is actually divine patience. In other
words, the delay in Christ's return is intentional,
providing an opportunity for those who have not
yet heard the gospel to hear, and those who have
not yet turned to Christ to trust in Him (2 Peter 3:9).

Nevertheless, while God's interest in the present age is genuine, it is also limited. A day will

come when all delays come to an end (Revelation 10:6). This time-bound period will give way to an age that is as everlasting as the God who created it. In view of this, it is essential that we make the most of the time that we have. Since the days are few, we cannot afford to squander them: "Be very careful, then, how you live—not as unwise but as wise, making the most of every opportunity, because the days are evil" (Ephesians 5:15).

We can redeem the time that remains by bringing glory to Jesus Christ, who is the focal point of all the ages. We can honor Him through our worship and encourage one another by our words. We can tell those who have not yet trusted in Him of their need to acknowledge Christ as Lord.

The following inscription is engraved over the sundial in Seaham Church of Durham, England:

> *The natural clock-work by the Mighty One*
> *Wound up at first, and ever since has gone:*
> *No pin drops out, its wheels and springs are good,*
> *It speaks its Maker's praise, though once it stood;*
> *But that was by order of the Workman's power;*
> *And when it stands again, it goes no more.*

This is a reminder to us that time is shorter than we realize. And when it is gone, it will take with it all the opportunity it once afforded to bring glory to Christ.

Lord of the Hours, thank You for the gift of this day. I consecrate it to You and pray that You would show me how to make the most of every moment. In thought, word, and deed, may everything I do "redeem the time." Amen.

20
GOD'S WORKMANSHIP

> For we are God's workmanship, created in
> Christ Jesus to do good works, which God pre-
> pared in advance for us to do. *(Ephesians 2:10)*

Bill studied art in college and had hoped to become
a commercial artist. But when his wife told him
she was going to have a baby, his life goals took an
unexpected turn. He dropped out of school and took
a job working on an assembly line for one of the major automobile companies. Although he had planned
to continue his studies at home and even produced
a few paintings, eventually Bill's brush, paints, and
easel ended up gathering dust in the basement. For
the rest of his life, Bill was haunted by the image of
pictures that he had never painted. At the end of
his life, Bill saw his existence as a blank canvas.

Although we may not realize it, we are part of a
great work of art. According to Ephesians 2:10, we
are "God's workmanship." In ancient Greek, this
term referred to a finished work. Literally, we are
God's "handiwork" or "that which is made" by God.
We are God's masterpiece, designed in love and
handcrafted by grace.

The fact that we are God's handiwork says as
much about the role of divine sovereignty in shap-
ing our lives as it does about divine artistry. Because
we have been created by God, He has the right to

order our lives: "You turn things upside down, as if the potter were thought to be like the clay! Shall what is formed say to him who formed it, 'He did not make me'? Can the pot say of the potter, 'He knows nothing'?" (Isaiah 29:16).

The work of God spoken of in Ephesians 2:10 is one of creation, but of a special kind of creation. Those who have undergone new birth in Jesus Christ have been created "to do good works." This statement is significant in view of its context. It follows on the heels of Paul's assertion that salvation is by grace and through faith, rather than by works, so that none may boast (Ephesians 2:8–9).

The biblical concept of grace is a dynamic one. Grace is an active principle in the believer's life. John Wesley once said that the best definition of Christianity he had ever heard was this: "Christianity is the life of God in the soul of man." Certainly, Christianity is a body of doctrines, a system of truth revealed in the Bible. But it is also true that Christianity is a relationship. All the blessings of the Christian life flow out of a personal relationship with Jesus Christ. But grace is also a life-giving principle and a dynamic power that transforms the life of the Christian and calls forth a response.

The popular hymn "Amazing Grace" was penned by John Newton, a former sea captain and slave trader. For Newton, "Amazing Grace" was more than a song. It was actually a testimony of his own personal experience of God's power to transform. In a series of letters to a friend, Newton compared the grace of God in the believer's life to the development of an ear of corn. It begins as a mere blade at the point of conversion. The Spirit of

God opens the blinded eyes of the sinner to see the need for eternal life in Christ. Next comes the ear. As the believer grows in assurance, he also grows in his understanding of what it means to be in Christ. This understanding has two dimensions. The believer begins to understand the depth of his own sinfulness and the deceitfulness of his own heart. At the same time, he knows that he is Christ's and that Christ is his. This assurance paves the way for the stage that Newton compared to the full ear of corn. In this stage, the believer is not as concerned about assurance but has one desire: to live for Christ.

One who has enjoyed the fully developed grace of the Christian life understands the role that works play in that experience. Works cannot save, but they are important because they reflect God's workmanship. We have been created by God, partly for the purpose of good works. Paul's use of the language of creation, however, also implies instrumentality. The good works of the Christian life are themselves a part of God's own creative work: "Therefore, if anyone is in Christ, he is a new creation; the old has gone, the new has come!" (2 Corinthians 5:17).

I have an illustration of this in my own home: I occasionally have trouble hanging up my clothes because I find that my closet is too crowded. The wardrobe that I actually wear is relatively small, but my difficulty stems from all the old clothes that I find difficult to throw out, even if they are hopelessly out of style when compared with today's fashions. There are a number of reasons for this: Out of sentimentality, I might keep the old jacket I wore on my first date with my wife, or I may keep a comfortable old shirt simply as a matter of habit.

While I may keep the old clothes that I no longer wear, when Jesus Christ enters the believer's life, He brings with Him an entirely new wardrobe of behavior. The Christian is commanded to "put on the new self." This "new self" has been created to be like God in true righteousness and holiness (Ephesians 4:24). We must set the old way of life aside, as one would an old set of clothes. This isn't always as easy as it sounds. Although we may be tempted by familiarity or habit to hang on to this old wardrobe, it has no place in our new lives. There is no need to live like the old self because God has provided a new self.

Pablo Picasso was once asked to paint a portrait of the well-known author Gertrude Stein. She came to the painter's studio and sat for several sessions, but eventually Picasso sent her away and finished the painting alone. When Miss Stein was shown the finished work, she complained that she did not look like that. "But you will" Picasso replied.

In the same way that Picasso's painting of Gertrude Stein was a reflection of what she would look like, we have an idea of what we will look like in Jesus Christ. The apostle Paul is telling us that we are a masterpiece, divinely crafted by the hand of God. In this case, however, the portrait is not one of us, but of the image of Christ, in whose image we have been created. For this reason, our lives do not have to be a blank canvas.

Creator God, create within me a clean heart and renew me after the image of Your Son. Enable me by the power of Your grace to do the good works that I was designed to do. Amen.

21

FELLOW CITIZENS
WITH GOD'S PEOPLE

Consequently, you are no longer foreigners and aliens, but fellow citizens with
God's people and members of God's household . . . . *(Ephesians 2:19)*

We usually don't think much about our own
citizenship. When the time comes to cross the bor-
der into another country, however, citizenship
becomes very important. On those occasions, the
country we call our own will determine which
rights and privileges we can enjoy.

Citizenship is also important in the Christian
life. Those of us who are a part of the church have
had our citizenship transferred into Christ's kingdom. As far as our relationship with God was
concerned, we were outsiders prior to our trusting
in Christ. So much so, in fact, that the Greek term
used by Paul to describe our former state is one that
means "to be estranged" or "to be alienated." In other passages, Paul uses even stronger language and
says that we were God's "enemies" (Romans 5:10).

Those to whom the book of Ephesians was
originally written were doubly excluded, since their
status as Gentiles also disqualified them from citizenship in Israel. Because they were "foreigners" to
God's people, they were unable to lay claim to the
promises related to God's covenants. Paul summarizes their condition by saying that they were

"without hope and without God in the world" (Ephesians 2:12).

Fortunately, something happened to change this. Those who were once far away from God were brought near by Jesus Christ. His death was the means God used to close the gap for those who had been alienated. It did this by removing the barrier that had separated them from God and from the rest of His people. This barrier was "the law with its commandments and regulations" (Ephesians 2:15).

In these passages, Paul expresses a tension that springs from two seemingly contradictory aspects of God's character. On one hand, they point to the reality of God's wrath against those who have broken His law. Their sin had alienated them from God and made them His enemies: "God is a righteous judge, a God who expresses his wrath every day" (Psalm 7:11). Those who are separated from Christ are separated from God and subject to His wrath. They are "condemned already" (John 3:18).

Despite this, God desires to reclaim those who are alienated from Him. While it is true that He cannot deny His own righteousness or change His standard without denying Himself, it is also true that He takes "no pleasure in the death of the wicked" (Ezekiel 33:11). Through the Cross, God was able to be true to both aspects of His nature without contradicting either. Because Christ fulfilled the law in every point, God did not need to lower His standard. Through His death, Christ became the object of divine wrath, suffering the penalty for those who had violated the law. In a single stroke, God's love and justice were combined to meet our need:

*For what the law was powerless to do in that it was
weakened by the sinful nature, God did by sending his
Son in the likeness of sinful man to be a sin offering. And
so he condemned sin in sinful man, in order that the
righteous requirements of the law might be fully met in
us, who do not live according to the sinful nature but according to the Spirit.* (Romans 8:3–4)

Christ's death was equally important for the Israelites who would believe in Him. The same
commandments and regulations that had separated
Jews from Gentiles inevitably condemned the Jews
who attempted to keep them. Since these laws were
designed to reflect God's own righteousness, perfect
obedience was the only standard that was acceptable to Him. This meant that even those who had
been given God's law as part of their national legacy
had been unable to keep it (Galatians 6:13). The
whole purpose of the law, then, was to show the
Gentiles their need for Christ and to lead Israel to
Him. The death of Jesus effectively removed the
barrier that had separated both the Jews and the
Gentiles from God and created an entirely new people known as the church. As a result, both Jews and
Gentiles can be citizens of Christ's kingdom by
faith.

What benefits do we receive because our citizenship now lies with Christ and His kingdom?
One of the most important is the right to be a resident. As citizens of Christ's kingdom, we have a
home with Him. He has promised that He will
come one day to claim us as His own, so that we
may be where He is (John 14:3; 17:24). But from
God's perspective, we are already seated with Christ
in heavenly places (Ephesians 2:6).

As citizens of Christ's kingdom, we also have a right to be protected by His power. The Bible tells us that through faith in Christ, we are "shielded by God's power" (1 Peter 1:5). Because we are the recipients of God's grace, we are protected from judgment and our salvation is assured. We are also protected from the power of Satan, as Christ has equipped us with the full armor of God, including the shield of faith "with which you can extinguish all the flaming arrows of the evil one" (Ephesians 6:16). Our hearts and minds are protected by the peace of God, as we share our concerns with Him in prayer (Philippians 4:6).

The rights of citizenship, however, also bring with them responsibility. As citizens of Christ's kingdom, we are obligated to set our minds on the things that pertain to it. We are to set our hearts on things above (Colossians 3:2). This means that we must put the interests of Christ's kingdom above all other interests, even our own. If we do so, God says He will see to it that our other concerns are met (Matthew 6:33).

Ordinarily citizenship brings with it certain rights. Citizenship in Christ's kingdom, however, may actually require that we set aside our rights for the sake of God's purposes. An American missionary couple who had just begun their term in Austria learned this lesson while waiting for a train. Seeing what they thought was a short cut, they ran across several tracks and arrived at the platform ahead of the rest of the waiting crowd, all of whom had taken the long way around. Once the missionaries were seated on the train, their host gently reproved them. "I know you didn't mean to," he explained, "but by cutting across the tracks, you offended everyone else who was waiting for the train. We just don't do that here."

Living in another culture is one of the best ways to discover the characteristics of one's own. Our experiences make us keenly aware of differences in core values and customs. This should also be true of those who belong to the kingdom of God. Each new day should make us more aware that our true citizenship lies with Jesus Christ and His kingdom.

Father, thank You for bridging the gap between Your justice and Your compassion with the blood of Christ. Make me more aware of where my true citizenship lies, as I set my heart upon things above this day. Amen.

22

PARTAKERS OF THE PROMISE

> This mystery is that through the gospel
> the Gentiles are heirs together with Israel,
> members together of one body, and sharers
> together in the promise in Christ Jesus.
> (*Ephesians 3:6*)

History is not everyone's favorite subject. Henry Ford is reputed to have said: "History is bunk." He felt that the only history that was really important was the history being made today. An inscription posted at the site of the Dachau concentration camp near Munich, Germany, expresses a different sentiment. It warns: "Those who do not learn from history are condemned to repeat its mistakes." To this we could add another: "Those who forget history are doomed to be ungrateful." This is especially true of spiritual history. The statement in Ephesians 3:6 that we are "sharers together in the promise in Christ Jesus" is a reminder of what we were and what we will be.

In this section of Scripture, the apostle Paul explains that God had made him caretaker of a "mystery" (Ephesians 3:3, 6). We usually think of a mystery as a puzzle that needs to be figured out. The reader of a mystery novel, for example, looks for clues that lead to the identification of the murderer. But when Paul uses the term *mystery* in the New Testament, he refers to something that had been previously known to God and is now made known to man. In this sense, a mystery is a form of revelation. If God had not revealed it by His Spirit, it would have remained hidden. The mystery Paul speaks of here, ". . . was not made known to men in other generations as it has now been revealed by the Spirit to God's holy apostles and prophets" (Ephesians 3:5).

God revealed to the apostles and prophets that the Gentiles had a part in the promises of God through Jesus Christ. This mystery is one that we now take for granted, but it means that Paul's mystery is also our history. Because God made this mystery known, we have a hope of heaven. If it had been kept hidden, Paul would never have been allowed to preach the gospel message to those who were not of Jewish descent. Had that been the case, the message would never have reached our ears, and we would still be destined for hell. Instead, we are partakers of "the promise."

This promise is one of life (2 Timothy 1:1). More specifically, it is the promise of *eternal* life: "And this is what he promised us—even eternal life" (1 John 2:25). It is also the promise of an eternal inheritance (Hebrews 9:15). It is the same promise made to the Old Testament saints and patriarchs, but which had to wait for the coming of Christ to find fulfillment: "These were all commended for their faith, yet none of them received what had been promised. God had planned something better for us so that only together with us would they be made perfect" (Hebrews 11:39–40). It is remarkable to consider that others had to wait so that we would not be left out.

In certain respects, however, we are in the

same position as our Old Testament ancestors in faith. They received tokens of the promise but waited for its ultimate fulfillment. Like them, we too received a token of the promise when we were given the Holy Spirit as a down payment or "deposit" guaranteeing our inheritance (Ephesians 1:13–14). We have received forgiveness through Christ: "But in keeping with his promise we are looking forward to a new heaven and a new earth, the home of righteousness" (2 Peter 3:13).

What will this new heaven and new earth be like? The Bible tells us that it will be familiar. It will still be the earth, and in many ways it will be like the earth we know today. According to the book of Revelation, it will contain plants, rivers, and even cities (Revelation 21–22; Luke 19:17, 19). But the new earth, upon which believers will live following the reign of Christ, will be just that—new!

The new heaven and new earth will be a challenging place to live. Jesus promised that those who trust in Him will also reign with Him (Revelation 3:21; cf. 2 Timothy 2:12). Although we do not know all that will be involved, the language used implies a measure of responsibility. We won't be floating on clouds all day and strumming harps. There will be meaningful work for us to do .We will continue to grow and develop in our obedience to Christ. Someone has said that the thing that most of us don't like about work is that it is so daily. There is always an element of drudgery, even in the best of jobs. This is a result of sin (Genesis 3:17–19). But in the new heaven and earth, the curse of sin will be removed, and with it the drudgery of daily work.

The most important characteristic of the new earth is that it will be "the home of righteousness" (2 Peter 3:13). At that time, all the brokenness that we see in this present world will be repaired. Our wounds will be healed, our broken hearts mended, and every tear dried.

As partakers of the promise, then, we stand in a unique position. Not only do we have the hope of the promise, we possess the promise itself. Paul makes it clear that the promise and all its benefits are encompassed in the person of Jesus Christ. While it is true that we look forward to the complete fulfillment of all that Jesus has promised, as those who share in Christ, we are already partakers of what He has promised (Hebrews 3:14).

The Bible is filled with promises that are the birthright of those who have placed their faith in God's Son. All of these promises find their ultimate fulfillment in Jesus Christ. Ultimately, He is the promise.

Dear Father, do not let me forget that I was once a stranger to the hope that I now have. Thank You for sending Your Son Jesus, who embodies all the promises of God. Amen.

23

THE BODY

> From him the whole body, joined and
> held together by every supporting ligament,
> grows and builds itself up in love, as each
> part does its work. *(Ephesians 4:16)*

Thomas Jefferson compared the human body to a
machine. In his old age, he wrote to John
Adams and said, ". . . our machines have now been
running seventy or eighty years, and we must expect that, worn as they are, here a pivot, there a
wheel, now a pinion, next a spring, will be giving
way; and however we may tinker them up for a
while, all will at length surcease their motion."

There was truth in what Jefferson wrote. The
body is like a machine in many ways. Its various
parts work together in a single purpose, and all are
directed by a brain that functions much like a com-
puter. Yet as good as Jefferson's analogy is, it falls
short in several ways. A machine does not direct itself. Its computerized "brain" must be programmed
by someone in order for it to function properly. A
machine performs its functions purposefully, but it
is a purpose determined by its designer. Moreover,
although a machine may be used to repair other
machines, it really does not repair itself.

The human body is so unique, in fact, that it is
the analogy that Scripture uses to help us understand the nature of the church. The church is the

body of Christ, with Jesus as its head and its various members functioning as joints and ligaments. This metaphor is used in Ephesians 4:3 to support Paul's teaching on the importance of keeping the unity of the Spirit in the bond of peace.

Unity among Christians is often emphasized today. There are even organizations whose purpose is to promote unity among various Christian groups and denominations. But what is most noticeable about Paul's teaching about Christian unity is that it emphasizes lifestyle rather than organization. In fact, Paul really does not urge Christians to unite. According to Ephesians 4:3, the unity of the Spirit is already a reality. Whether or not we like it, we are united with everyone else who is in Jesus Christ.

Paul's concern is not whether there will be unity in the church but whether that unity will be maintained in the bond of peace. Believers can be bound together in peace, or they can be bound together in their dislike for one another. It is clear that peace among the members of the body of Christ is not automatic. It must be preserved.

Three factors contribute to the unity of the church. One factor is the character of God. The Bible teaches that the one true God exists in a single essence as three distinct persons. There is "one Spirit," "one Lord," and "one God and Father of all who is over all and through all and in all" (Ephesians 4:4–6). Although this concept is difficult to grasp, it is a fundamental teaching of the Christian faith. The unity of the Godhead is reflected in the makeup of the church. In fact, Jesus prayed for this very thing in the garden of Gethsemane (John 17:20–21).

The second contributing factor to the unity of the church is a common spiritual experience. All believers are united in their hope of eternal life and in their experience of being joined to Christ by the Holy Spirit (Ephesians 4:5–7). Churches have many different methods of receiving new members. Some are elaborate. For example, the candidate may be asked to go through a lengthy catechism class or screening process. Other churches are more simple. If you walk up the aisle at the end of the service, you automatically become a member of that church. When it comes to joining the body of Christ, however, everybody must enter the same way. Each one must come by faith in Jesus Christ to receive the grace of God. Although the times and circumstances of conversion differ for each, the spiritual mechanics are the same for everybody.

The third factor that contributes to the unity of the church is a common doctrine. In Ephesians 4:5 Paul says that all those who are part of the body of Christ share "one faith." Although Paul often uses this term to speak of the need for personal trust in the saving work of Christ, in this case he is referring to "the faith"—the body of teachings that comprise the church's doctrine. One of the ironies of today's emphasis on church unity is the tendency to downplay the importance of biblical doctrine. Those who hold this view assert that what the world needs most is to see those who profess to be Christians getting together for worship or community action. "Ignore the differences in doctrine," they recommend. "Focus instead on those issues upon which we all agree." True biblical unity, however, is founded on a system of belief. Without sound doctrine, the church's unity is just a sham. It is purely cosmetic.

Although the biblical analogy of the body points to the unity that all believers share in Christ, it also underscores the diversity that exists among those who are in the church. Just as the human body has many members, each with its own unique function, every believer performs a distinct role in the body of Christ: "The body is a unit, though it is made up of many parts; and though all its parts are many, they form one body. So it is with Christ" (1 Corinthians 12:12).

When we violate this principle, we usually do so in two ways. One way is to see ourselves as unnecessary to the healthy functioning of the church. This is often due to a sense of inferiority. Since we do not have many gifts, or the gifts that we have do not seem remarkable, we conclude that we are not essential (1 Corinthians 12:15–16). The other way that we violate this principle is by competing with the other members of the body (1 Corinthians 12:21). When this happens, the church engages in what might be described as a "beauty contest," giving preference to those whose gifts are more spectacular. In reality, every member contributes to the operation of the body as a whole. Even those whose gifts seem unimpressive are essential to the health of the church (1 Corinthians 12:23–24).

There is one sense in which Thomas Jefferson's words about the human body are all too true. Despite the wonder of its design and the interworking of its parts, no matter how much we tinker with it, in time it will cease to function. The body's capacity to heal itself is limited. But the opposite is true of the church. The body of Christ will build itself up "until we all reach unity in the faith and in the knowledge of the Son of God and become mature, attaining to the whole measure of the fullness of Christ" (Ephesians 4:13).

Head of the Church, I am grateful that Your Spirit has made me a part of the body of Christ. Open my eyes to see the value of my own ministry and the importance of all those who work together with me to build up the church. Amen.

24

IMITATORS OF GOD

Be imitators of God, therefore, as dearly
loved children . . . . (*Ephesians 5:1*)

Some have called imitation "the sincerest form of
flattery." In the Christian life, however, it is an
important principle of discipleship. This is not surprising, since imitation is a basic component of the
learning process. A child learns to speak by mimic-
king the sounds we hear from our parents. We
learn to write by copying letters. Apprentices ob-
serve the skills of others in order to learn their craft.
In the same way, those who are followers of Jesus
Christ are commanded to "imitate" God.

But how, exactly, do we carry this out? We do
this by following Jesus' example. Ephesians 5:2 explains that we are to ". . . live a life of love, just as
Christ loved us and gave himself up for us as a fra-
grant offering and sacrifice to God." During the
Jesus movement of the '60s and '70s, many of us
thought that this verse meant that we should greet
one another with a warm hug. Although there was
nothing wrong with this practice, it missed the real
essence of this command. The essence of love is not
emotion but self-sacrifice.

Christ gave us the supreme example of sacrificial love when He "gave himself up for us." The

Greek term for this literally means "to hand over." Interestingly, this is the same term used to describe the action of Judas Iscariot, the one who handed Jesus over to His enemies to be crucified (Matthew 10:4). The same word is used in Matthew 27:26, which says that after Pontius Pilate had Jesus flogged, he "handed him over to be crucified."

Ultimately, however, Jesus gave Himself up when he surrendered Himself to death. By becoming a sacrifice, He showed us what it means to walk in love. This one-time offering on the cross was really the culmination of an entire ministry of self-sacrifice. Jesus gave Himself up for others on a daily basis. At times, this meant explaining the gospel to social outcasts, even when He was tired, hungry, and thirsty (John 4:1–42). On other occasions, it meant spending His time ministering to the crowd that had followed Him to the secluded spot where He had hoped to find some privacy (Matthew 14:13–14). It meant healing the multitudes, even when He knew that they would never thank Him or follow Him as Savior (Luke 17:17–18).

If we are a part of God's family, we will follow Christ's example. We will put others first, sacrificing ourselves for them just as Christ sacrificed Himself for us. There are both negative and positive implications in this. Negatively, it means that there are certain things that we will not do. For example, we are not to be ruled by impurity or greed. No believer should have a reputation for being immoral (Ephesians 5:3). While there may have been instances of immorality in his past, the believer's present should be radically different (1 Corinthians 6:9–11). No believer should be known for having a foul mouth. The moral character of our lives should be so evident that it is reflected in our everyday speech: "Nor should there be obscenity, foolish talk, or coarse joking, which are out of place, but rather thanksgiving" (Ephesians 5:4). And no one should be able to point at a believer and say, "There goes a greedy person."

The problem with the actions Paul condemns in Ephesians 5:3–4 is not they are embarrassing but that they are a contradiction. They are a denial of our spiritual heritage in Jesus Christ: "For of this you can be sure: No immoral, impure or greedy person—such a man is an idolater—has any inheritance in the kingdom of Christ and of God" (Ephesians 5:5). Everywhere the Christian goes, he or she leaves behind a trail of actions that show whether or not there is a "family resemblance" to Christ.

Positively then, the principle of imitating Christ is founded upon the knowledge that the believer's life is ruled by the power of grace. We are not expected to mimic the life of Jesus by following Him in our own strength. Paul's command to follow the example of Jesus is grounded in the fact that we have become God's offspring through Christ. There is more to this relationship than birthright; there is real spiritual power: "No one who is born of God will continue to sin, because God's seed remains in him; he cannot go on sinning, because he has been born of God" (1 John 3:9). Only those who have been born of God are capable of acting as "dearly loved children" (Ephesians 5:1).

Does this mean that the true Christian will never lapse into any of these areas of sin? This seems unlikely. If practices like these had not been a real danger for genuine Christians, Paul would not have felt compelled to warn against them. The repeated warnings of Scripture that Christians should turn away from such behavior indicate that the believers of the New Testament era struggled with these practices to the same degree that we do. It is just as clear, however, that the standard we are to measure our lives by is Jesus Christ.

J. C. Ryle, who was appointed Bishop of Liverpool by nineteenth century British Prime Minister Benjamin Disraeli, noted that holiness is an essential trait for those who are bound for heaven: "I know not what others may think, but it does seem clear that heaven would be a miserable place to an unholy man." The kingdom of God will only admit a certain kind of citizen. Those who are a part of Christ's kingdom are not natural-born citizens, but those who have been supernaturally born. For this reason Ryle warns: "Boast not of Christ's work for you, unless you can show the Spirit's work in you."

Heavenly Father, I pray that my life today will give evidence of the Holy Spirit's transforming work. By His power I determine to follow Christ's example and walk as a child of God. Amen.

25

CHILDREN OF LIGHT

> For you were once darkness, but now you
> are light in the Lord. Live as children of
> light. (*Ephesians 5:8*)

The dynamic of grace shapes our personal rela-
tionships as much as it does our behavior. Since
no immoral, greedy, or impure person has any inheritance in the kingdom of God, Christ's followers
should not be "partners" with such people (Ephesians 5:7). This is the same word Paul used to
describe believers in Ephesians 3:6, where it refers
to believers as "sharers together in the promise in
Christ Jesus." Those who are "sharers together" in
Christ should not share in the actions of those who
are alienated from Him.

The reason for this is twofold. First, we should
not be partners in this kind of behavior because it is
displeasing to God (Ephesians 5:6). On a more fundamental level, however, we are to behave differently
because we *are* different.

Paul uses the contrast of light and darkness in
Ephesians 5:8 to illustrate the difference between
those who belong to Christ and those who do not.
Throughout the New Testament, the present world
is described as being in a state of darkness. For example, John 1:5 says that when the "light" of Jesus'
life shone in the realm of darkness, it was not un-

derstood. Also, the world condemned itself by loving darkness more than light (John 3:19). And Jesus' enemies handed Him over to be crucified because they operated under the domain of darkness (Luke 22:53).

Christ, however, has removed us from the control of this realm and transferred us into the kingdom of light: "For he has rescued us from the dominion of darkness and brought us into the kingdom of the Son he loves, in whom we have redemption, the forgiveness of sins" (Colossians 1:13–14).

This darkness was more than an environment in which we lived prior to the entrance of Christ into our lives. According to Paul, before we trusted in Christ, we *were* darkness. The deepest core of our being was controlled by the power of sin. We may have been very religious; it is even possible that we lived a life of exemplary morality. The Bible says that Paul's own life before his encounter with the resurrected Jesus on the Damascus road was unparalleled (Philippians 3:4–7). Unfortunately, all his moral achievements—even his own sincere desire to do right—could not change the fact that there was another influence in Paul's heart constantly working against his best intentions. He characterized this influence as "the law of sin" and wrote: "For in my inner being I delight in God's law; but I see another law at work in the members of my body, waging war against the law of my mind and making me a prisoner of the law of sin at work within my members" (Romans 7:22–23).

The Cross has changed this. The light of Christ now shines in our hearts (2 Corinthians 4:6). We no longer belong to the darkness but are "sons of the light" (1 Thessalonians 5:5). Since God is Himself light, our status as children of God obligates us to walk as children of light (1 John 1:6–7). According to Ephesians 5:8–9, this is a matter of producing the fruit of goodness, righteousness, and truth. The language of fruit bearing points to God's role in this process. We can walk as children of light because the Holy Spirit is at work reproducing God's own character in us.

While the ability to walk in the light requires dependency upon God, we still must make a deliberate decision to do so. There is even an element of exploration as we "find out what pleases the Lord," a command that implies that such knowledge is not automatic (Ephesians 5:10). Paul literally says that we are to "test" the things that are pleasing to God. Fortunately, we have something more reliable than trial and error at our disposal for this. In order to bring to light the things that please God, we must have our minds renewed (Romans 12:2). The two primary instruments God uses to do this are the anointing of His Spirit and the teaching of His Word.

The Holy Spirit functions as an internal instructor (1 John 2:20, 27). The Scriptures provide us with a written record of what "pleases" God (1 John 3:22), and the internal testimony of the Spirit never contradicts God's written testimony. Both work in concert with one another in the believer's life. God has also gifted the church with individuals who have the ability to teach and whose ministry equips believers for obedience (Ephesians 4:11–12).

Although we ourselves are no longer a part of

the domain of darkness, we continue to have a responsibility to those who are. One of the chief characteristics of light is its ability to illuminate what is hidden in darkness. As children of light, we "expose" the fruitless deeds of darkness (Ephesians 5:11). This is what John the Baptist did when he reproved Herod for marrying his brother's wife (Matthew 14:3–4). He uncovered Herod's behavior and revealed its true nature. Like John's preaching, a life fully committed to Jesus Christ can serve as a "wake-up call" to those who are still in the grip of darkness (Ephesians 5:14).

It is easy to see how such a responsibility calls for discernment. When it comes to confronting others with their sin and their need for Christ, we have many strategies at our disposal. In some cases, direct confrontation is the best method. Others respond to mercy (Jude 23). We need to know how to make the most of each opportunity that comes along (Ephesians 5:15). The improper approach may cause us to squander an opportunity that will never come again.

This kind of discernment can only come as insight from the Holy Spirit. Therefore, it is essential that we be "filled" with the Spirit (Ephesians 5:18). We have already received the Holy Spirit as part of our birthright as God's children, but we need to continually yield to His control (Romans 8:9). To help us understand how this works, Paul contrasts the influence of the Holy Spirit with that of wine. When someone becomes drunk on wine, there is a chemical reaction in the brain that results in a loss of control. The power to reason, the ability to react, and the capacity for self-control are all affected. The

Holy Spirit affects these same areas, but in a different way. The Holy Spirit also operates on the mind, but the effect is rational and spiritual rather than chemical. The Holy Spirit affects the believer's ability to react and the capacity for reason and self-control. Instead of inhibiting these areas, as alcohol does, the Spirit stimulates them. It is the Holy Spirit who takes the knowledge we gain as we read the Bible and enables us to apply it to our circumstances. The Holy Spirit does not cause us to lose control but produces the fruit of self-control (Galatians 5:22–23).

Those who live as children of light also have a mutual responsibility to one another. They are to "Speak to one another with psalms, hymns and spiritual songs . . ." (Ephesians 5:19). These activities are congregational in nature. One implication of this command is that those who wish to be controlled by the Spirit also need to worship with God's people. This is a foundational principle in the Christian life. It is simply impossible to have a healthy Christian life while neglecting corporate worship. Even if we maintain our personal disciplines of prayer and Bible study, we still need to meet with God's people. Life in the Spirit will produce life in the body of Christ.

Paul's command also underscores our need to be directed by the Holy Spirit when we gather for worship. It is important to remember that we serve as God's mouthpiece when we interact with others. The Holy Spirit is also an important factor in the overall attitude of the church. A church full of grumbling and complaining is a hindrance to the gospel. It is unlikely that we will be able to attract unbelievers to Christ if we are constantly criticizing one another.

We are called to live as children of light, but we are not called to do it alone. This responsibility is placed upon the whole church. Living as children of light is a group effort.

Light of the World, shine through Your church in a way that will enable others to see our love. Help me to live as a child of the Light. Amen.

26

A RADIANT CHURCH

> Husbands, love your wives, just as Christ loved the church and gave himself up for her to make her holy, cleansing her by the washing with water through the word, and to present her to himself as a radiant church, without stain or wrinkle or any other blemish, but holy and blameless. *(Ephesians 5:25–27)*

The bride stood at the front of the church, holding tightly to her father's arm: She smiled shyly at the groom and looked expectantly toward the pastor. "Who gives this woman to be married to this man?" the pastor asked. The nervous father's reply was barely audible. He said in a trembling voice, "Her mother and I." Then he placed his daughter's hand gently in the groom's, kissed her, and wiped away a tear as he turned toward the pew where his wife was waiting.

This scene has been replayed countless times in weddings from generation to generation. Traditionally, it is the parents who have presented the bride to the bridegroom. This was also true in New Testament times. In Jesus' day, a betrothal gift was given by the parents, and the bride was led to the groom's home in a procession (Matthew 25:1–13). The scene will be slightly different, however, when the bride of Christ is joined to her Lord. At that time, according to Ephesians 5:27, the bride of Christ will be presented "as a radiant church" by Jesus Himself.

In the original text, the term *radiant* literally means "glorious." Glory is one of the attributes of God. He is called the "King of glory" in Psalm 24:7 and the "God of glory" in Psalm 29:3. God shows His glory through what He has done. God's glory is evident in creation (Psalm 19:1). According to Psalm 96:3, He declares His glory among the nations through His "marvelous deeds." However, God's' glory is most clearly revealed in Jesus Christ (John 1:14).

This glory was a reflection of the Father's glory, possessed by Jesus before the world began and fully restored to Him after His resurrection (John 17:5). Jesus is: ". . . the image of the invisible God, the firstborn over all creation" (Colossians 1:15).

Like Jesus, our ancestor Adam once reflected the Father's glory. Prior to the fall, he was created in "the image of God" (Genesis 1:26–27). One of the consequences of Adam's sin was that it caused him and all who came after him to "fall short" of God's glory (Romans 3:23). As a result of sin's blinding effect, humanity exchanged the glory of God and recast it in the image of the things that God Himself had created (Romans 1:25). Those who come to know Christ by faith regain the knowledge of this glory (2 Corinthians 4:6).

God is protective of His glory (Exodus 34:14). This is not because He is "jealous" in a human sense but because He is aware of His own uniqueness. In Isaiah 42:8, we are warned: "I am the Lord; that is my name! I will not give my glory to another or my praise to idols" (cf. Isaiah 48:11). Yet despite this, the Scriptures promise that when Christ presents us to Himself, we will share in His glory to such an extent that we will *be* glorious.

This new status springs from two actions of Christ. It is rooted first in the fact that Jesus loved us with a love that was reflected in His actions when He "gave himself up" for us. This is the language of sacrifice and refers to His work on the cross (Ephesians 5:2). Secondly, Christ cleansed us "by the washing with water through the word" (Ephesians 5:26). Together, these provide the basis for our sanctification. Christ's death was a single and unrepeatable event that reversed the effect of sin and provided a righteous standing for those who had fallen short of God's standard. The washing of the word is an ongoing process that God uses to transform our minds and guide our actions, as we rely upon the power of the Holy Spirit to obey its directives. As a result of both, we will stand before Christ on the day of judgment genuinely holy and without blame, an unblemished bride who has no stain or wrinkle.

It is important to note that what Paul has to say in this verse is more than abstract theology. These words provide the foundation for a very practical command: "Husbands, love your wives, just as Christ loved the church . . . ." The husband who would love his wife as God intended must have a clear understanding of the work of Christ. If he thinks of love in a purely worldly sense, he may look at this command and say, "I have loving feelings for my wife; I must be doing all right." Or the opposite may be true, and he may say, "I don't have any feelings for my wife, so I can't obey this command." In reality, though, biblical love is demonstrated in action.

The husband who loves his wife as Christ loved the church will be available for her and sensitive to her needs. Availability means that his wife will have regular access to him. Unfortunately, his physical presence is not always a guarantee of this. A husband who is truly available has also learned how to listen and communicate. A sensitive husband understands the needs of his wife. He has learned how to live with his wife "in an understanding way" (1 Peter 3:7 NASB).

Because the marriage bond reflects the relationship between Christ and the church, there is more at stake in our obedience to Paul's command than mere happiness (Ephesians 5:32). Ultimately, Christian marriage is a form of witness and a method of instruction. It provides a world that has been blinded by sin with a living analogy of the love of Christ.

The bride is not the only one who is given away at the marriage ceremony. By promising to love his wife as Christ loves the Church, the groom gives himself to the bride. A cynic has called marriage an institution where "a man gives up privileges he never realized he had." In reality, the husband gives up much more. He gives up his very life. When Jesus loved, He gave up Himself. The husband who follows Christ's example can do no less.

Lord Jesus, thank You for giving up Your life for me. Show me the opportunities You have placed before me today to follow in Your steps. I will give myself to You as I give myself to others. Amen.

27

THE TRUE CIRCUMCISION

> Watch out for those dogs, those men who
> do evil, those mutilators of the flesh. For it is
> we who are the circumcision, we who
> worship by the Spirit of God, who glory in
> Christ Jesus, and who put no confidence in
> the flesh . . . .(Philippians 3:2–3)

The church at Philippi, a Macedonian city located on the major shipping route known as the
Via Egnatia, had a problem with dogs. Not with the
kind that are furry and have a tail, but with two-
legged dogs. In his concluding warnings to the
Philippian believers, the apostle Paul warned them:
"Watch out for those dogs, those men who do evil,
those mutilators of the flesh" (Philippians 3:2).

The church in Philippi began with the conversion of Lydia, a Gentile businesswoman who had
become a proselyte to Judaism. She first heard the
gospel when Paul preached to a group of women
who had gathered near a river outside the city to
pray (Acts 16:13–15). The fact that they were meet-
ing by the riverside indicates that there was no
synagogue and suggests that the Jewish population
of Philippi was quite small. The growth of the
church, however, drew the attention of Jews, including those who had come to Antioch and
taught: "Unless you are circumcised, according to
the custom taught by Moses, you cannot be saved"
(Acts 15:1).

Paul's description of these teachers as "dogs" was intended to be ironic. This word was often used by the Jews to speak of the Gentiles (Psalm 22:16). Jesus used it Himself to refer to a woman from Syrian Phoenicia who came to Him and begged Him to drive a demon out of her daughter: "'First let the children eat all they want,' he told her, 'for it is not right to take the children's bread and toss it to their dogs.' 'Yes, Lord,' she replied, 'but even the dogs under the table eat the children's crumbs'" (Mark 7:27–28). Jesus was so impressed by the faith demonstrated in the woman's quick-witted reply that He granted her request.

The "dogs" of Philippi, though, were false teachers who were attempting to infiltrate the church. In calling them this, Paul was probably using their own language against them. They called uncircumcised Gentile Christians "dogs," implying that they were not truly a part of God's people.

Paul's evaluation of their doctrine is evident in the harsh language he used to characterize them. He described them as "men who do evil." This is somewhat ironic, in view of the fact that they were probably meticulous in their observance of the rituals and traditions of rabbinical Judaism. Paul's description was justified, however, because these men taught that the way to be saved was by keeping the Law and doing good works. But because they were not trusting in Christ, the works that seemed good in their own eyes were really evil since they were a form of self-righteousness.

Paul also characterized them as "those mutilators of the flesh," an allusion to their emphasis on the rite of circumcision. Originally practiced by many Semitic nations, circumcision was introduced to Israel when God commanded Abraham to be circumcised as a sign of the covenant that He had made with him (Genesis 17:1–14). For Abraham, the rite of circumcision was ". . . a seal of the righteousness he had by faith while he was still uncircumcised" (Romans 4:11). For Abraham's descendants, it was a reminder of God's promise that He would also declare them righteous if they followed in the steps of Abraham's faith.

It is clear from a number of Old Testament passages that circumcision had a symbolic meaning. In Deuteronomy 10:16, for example, God's people were told: "Circumcise your hearts, therefore, and do not be stiff-necked any longer." Similarly, the prophet Jeremiah explained to those in the kingdom of Judah that in order to truly circumcise themselves to the Lord, they would need to circumcise their hearts (Jeremiah 4:4). The ritual of circumcision pointed to the need for a spiritual change, but it could not bring about that change.

Paul explained the difference between those who were "truly" circumcised and those who were only circumcised in the flesh by pointing out:

> A man is not a Jew if he is only one outwardly, nor is circumcision merely outward and physical. No, a man is a Jew if he is one inwardly; and circumcision is circumcision of the heart, by the Spirit, not by the written code. Such a man's praise is not from men, but from God. (Romans 2:28–29)

From God's perspective, then, being a physical descendant of Abraham did not automatically guarantee that one was a true heir to the righteousness promised to Abraham. Only those who shared Abraham's faith could be called "Jews" in the true sense of the word. The outward sign of circumcision meant nothing if there was no spiritual reality behind it.

Those who have trusted in Jesus Christ live in the spiritual reality that circumcision was meant to picture:

> *In him you were also circumcised, in the putting off of the sinful nature, not with a circumcision done by the hands of men but with the circumcision done by Christ, having been buried with him in baptism and raised with him through your faith in the power of God, who raised him from the dead.* (Colossians 2:11–12)

In Christ, it is the life of the Spirit that counts. We have no confidence in the flesh because we know that the flesh lacks the power to please God (Romans 7:18). We do not trust in mere ritual to please God but worship Him through the empowerment of the Holy Spirit. Paul's words, though blunt, are both an encouragement and a warning. They offer confidence to those who are bold enough to trust in Christ alone. At the same time, they are a warning to those who depend upon their religious heritage or human effort to gain acceptance in God's sight. The work of Christ alone is sufficient to justify. Anything else that is added to it, even if it is religious in nature, is, in fact, defiling.

God of Israel, I claim Christ alone as my righteousness. Circumcise my heart and make it responsive to You. Amen.

28

BRETHREN

And we urge you, brothers, warn those who
are idle, encourage the timid, help the weak, be
patient with everyone. (*1 Thessalonians 5:14*)

According to the old saying, blood is thicker
than water. In reality, however, family members
tend to take one another for granted. Years of living
together on a daily basis can blind us to the
strengths of those we love and make us overly
aware of their flaws. The same can be true of the
church. That is why the apostle Paul found it necessary to remind the Thessalonians of their obligation
to treat one another as "brethren."

Those of us who have been joined to Jesus
Christ by faith have also been joined to one another. Our common faith has made us brothers and
sisters in Christ. Our calling in Christ is a call to
freedom, but to a particular kind of freedom: the
freedom to "serve one another in love" (Galatians
5:13).

What exactly do we owe one another as members of God's family? In 1 Thessalonians 5:14 the
apostle identifies the three primary responsibilities
of the family: We are to warn those who are idle,
encourage those who are timid, and help those who
are weak. These responsibilities are each an out-
growth of the more general command to "live in

peace with each other" (1 Thessalonians 5:13). Peace in the church does not come when we ignore other believers. Being a part of God's family means that we are to be accountable to one another.

Like any family, those who are in God's family occasionally need to be disciplined. As members of the family of God, we are called to "admonish" the unruly. This term is actually a compound word made up of the Greek term for "mind" and the verb "to put." Therefore, when we admonish, we touch the mind. Admonition is a form of instruction and implies that correction is needed. True admonition, however, does more than merely point out what is wrong. It also provides direction.

Who needs this kind of redirection? According to Paul, it is especially for the "idle," or more literally, those who are "without order." The King James Version translates this word as "unruly." Although idleness is a condition that requires correction, the people Paul had in mind here were not merely lazy, but troublemakers as well. These busybodies continually stirred up trouble in the congregation (2 Thessalonians 3:11). The responsibility to admonish such people was one shared by all believers (Romans 15:14), and those who refused to listen to correction were to be avoided (2 Thessalonians 3:6).

Not everyone in the family of God should be dealt with the same way. While some need to be admonished, others need to be encouraged. Admonition is for the irresponsible, but encouragement is for the fearful. To some extent, encouragement is more positive than admonition. Admonition assumes that correction is needed, while encouragement is designed to comfort. When I admonish, I function as a coach. When I encourage, I act as a cheerleader.

For some, however, words of encouragement are simply not enough. They need something more practical. Paul's directive for dealing with these believers is to "help the weak." The picture in Paul's mind is that of standing opposite someone and holding them up. The irresponsible need to be told to straighten up, the fearful need to be cheered up, but weak believers need to be propped up.

Why not simply leave the weak to fend for themselves? We have an obligation to support the weak because Christ helped us when we were unable to help ourselves (Romans 5:6). Because of this, "we who are strong ought to bear with the failings of the weak and not to please ourselves" (Romans 15:1).

When Paul speaks of weak believers, he is usually referring to those who suffered from a "weak" conscience. Unlike those Paul describes as "strong," the weak were bound by their personal convictions to refrain from activities that other Christians saw as harmless. They would not eat certain foods that they considered unclean and refused to eat foods that had been sacrificed to idols (Romans 14:1–2; 1 Corinthians 8:7). They regarded certain days as more sacred than others, while "stronger" believers considered every day alike. The biblical principle of supporting the weak demanded that those with the stronger consciences accept those whose faith was weak without condemning them (Romans 14:1–23).

Bob had always been a fan of country western music. He taught himself how to play guitar and made it his life's goal to sing on the stage of the "Grand Ol' Opry." After he came to know Christ, however, he realized that this style of music had become a kind of idol in his life. Although Bob continued to play the guitar and sing after he was saved, he decided that he would play gospel music only. Bob started attending church and began to use his musical ability in the Sunday school class. However, when his Sunday school teacher learned of his convictions about country western music, he became upset, concluding that Bob was being too "legalistic." Week after week, he urged Bob to ignore the convictions of his overly sensitive conscience and return to playing country-western music. Although he had good intentions, Bob's teacher had missed the point of Paul's directive. It is the strong who are to adapt to the weak.

In every case, whether we are admonishing the idle, encouraging the timid, or helping the weak, we must put the other person first. We cannot afford to think only of ourselves. This is a cardinal rule in any family, and it is especially true of the family of God. Where the church is concerned, you can't spell "brothers" without spelling "others."

Heavenly Father, thank You for making me a part of Your family. Make me sensitive to the needs of my brothers and sisters and equip me to meet those needs. Amen.

29
GOD'S HOUSEHOLD

> Although I hope to come to you soon, I am
> writing you these instructions so that, if I am
> delayed, you will know how people ought to
> conduct themselves in God's household, which
> is the church of the living God, the pillar and
> foundation of the truth. *(1 Timothy 3:14–15)*

Many large corporations publish what they call
an "employee's guide" or an "employee's hand-
book." This manual provides detailed information
about how the company operates. In essence, it
serves as a kind of corporate rule book. The church
has a similar manual. The New Testament outlines
the principles by which the church is to operate.
While the entire Bible has bearing on the life of the
church, the pastoral epistles, including the book of
1 Timothy, provide specific instructions about its
organizational structure, policies, and practices.
According to 1 Timothy 3:15, one of the reasons
Paul wrote this epistle was so that Timothy would
know how to conduct himself in the "God's household."

The Greek term that is translated "household"
often refers to a dwelling place or house. The
phrase "house of God" is frequently used in reference to the tabernacle and the temple (Exodus
23:19; Deuteronomy 23:18; 1 Chronicles 9:13;
Matthew 12:4). It can also refer to a group of people. When it is used in this latter sense, it often

means "family" (Genesis 17:23; Acts 10:2). At times, both senses are combined. Hebrews 3:4–5 notes that, "every house is built by someone, but God is the builder of everything" and then characterizes Moses as being "faithful as a servant in all God's house."

In 1 Timothy 3:14–15, Paul combines both ideas when referring to the church. It is the household, or family, of God. Consequently, many of the principles that are true of the family also hold true in the church. For example, those who exercise leadership in the church must also have a proven record of leadership in the home: "If anyone does not know how to manage his own family, how can he take care of God's church?" (1 Timothy 3:5; cf. 3:12).

Like any family, God's household has an authority structure. Those who serve as elders exercise "oversight" over God's people and "shepherd" them like a flock (1 Peter 5:1–2). As shepherds, the church's elders provide guidance for God's people. The typical member of the church is focused primarily on the present. The elder is interested in the present but is also equally concerned with the church's future. Without a clear sense of direction, the elder will be driven by the flock as it scatters in every direction.

The church's elders also provide protection. When Paul gave instructions to the elders of the church of Ephesus, he charged them: "Keep watch over yourselves and all the flock of which the Holy Spirit has made you overseers. Be shepherds of the church of God, which he bought with his own blood" (Acts 20:28).

The elders protect the church from threats that come from the outside by guarding against false teachers and false doctrine. They also guard the church from threats that come from inside the church by holding the flock accountable. When they see God's people straying in their Christian lives, part of their responsibility is to guide them back to the proper path. At times, this can be a painful process. Just as the Palestinian shepherd had to use his staff to prod the sheep, the elder must sometimes use the Word of God and the process of church discipline to goad erring believers.

The work of an elder is difficult. It is time-consuming and can be discouraging. An elder often finds that God's people are unresponsive to his efforts to steer them back to a more biblical path of life. The danger in such circumstances is that the elder will develop a grudging spirit.

The apostle Peter warned elders not to shepherd the flock under compulsion but to accept the responsibility voluntarily. He also warned of the danger of approaching this task with mixed motives:

> Be shepherds of God's flock that is under your care, serving as overseers—not because you must, but because you are willing, as God wants you to be; not greedy for money, but eager to serve; not lording it over those entrusted to you, but being examples to the flock. (1 Peter 5:2–3)

Because spiritual leaders often have access to the church's funds, greed is a real danger. However, we might also expand this warning to include other forms of gain. For example, it could include those who aspire to positions of leadership in the flock because of pride or because they wish to control the church.

There is authority in spiritual leadership, but it is the authority of a servant. Those who serve as elders in the church function as caretakers rather than kings. They are to be examples rather than emperors.

The church is a family, but it is also a temple. In addition to being "the household of God," it is "the pillar and foundation of the truth." It is important to carefully note Paul's wording. He is not merely saying that the church is founded on the truth. The church is built upon the foundation of Jesus Christ, who is the gospel proclaimed by the apostles (1 Corinthians 3:11; Ephesians 2:20). The gospel is called "the word of truth" (Colossians 1:5). In 1 Timothy 3:15, however, Paul says that the church is itself the pillar and foundation of the truth. It could be said that the truth is as dependent upon the church as the church is upon the truth. The church is a support to the truth because it has been entrusted with the gospel and has been given the responsibility of preserving and communicating it.

The church is both the household of God and the house of God. Its members comprise God's family, and God Himself dwells in their midst. It is both the place where God is worshiped and the repository of divine truth. We cannot protect this truth if we refuse to live by it.

Heavenly Father, instruct me through Your Word so that I know what is expected of me as a part of Your household. Teach me by Your truth so that I can truly be its pillar and support. Amen.

30

A PEOPLE THAT ARE HIS VERY OWN

> . . . while we wait for the blessed hope—the glorious appearing of our great God and Savior, Jesus Christ, who gave himself for us to redeem us from all wickedness and to purify for himself a people that are his very own, eager to do what is good. *(Titus 2:13–14)*

The trophy was old and slightly tarnished. Its name plate, identifying the original owner and the event for which it had been awarded, was no longer attached. But when my five-year-old son Jarred saw it sitting among the other worthless items at a local garage sale, he had to have it for his own.

"It's only a quarter," he told me excitedly. He had robbed his piggy bank of its change and had come to the garage sale hoping to find some old toys at a good price. He paid the money and eagerly took the trophy, cradling it in his lap all the way home.

As soon as we pulled in the driveway, he jumped out of the car and rushed into the house. Setting the trophy down for a better look, he took two steps back, placed his hands on his hips, and contemplated his new purchase for several minutes.

"I'll bet some day you'll have a trophy of your very own, Jarred," I said.

"But Dad," he objected, looking at me with a smile so radiant that you would have thought a judge awarded him the trophy that morning, "I already have a trophy!"

The trophy was his. He had bought and paid for it. Two years later, it was still sitting on his dresser, next to his Little League trophies.

In the same way that Jarred bought that trophy for himself, Jesus purchased the church as "a people for his very own" (Titus 2:14). The idea behind this phrase is that of a special possession of considerable value. We are Christ's treasure, made precious by the price that He paid in order to redeem us. This same verse tells us that Jesus offered Himself as the ransom on our behalf, purchasing us from "all wickedness."

As a result, we are Christ's trophies, on display as living testimonies to God's grace. According to Titus 2:11, this grace has "appeared to all men," a reference to Christ's first coming. The Greek term that is translated "appeared" in this verse is one from which the word "epiphany" comes. In ancient Greek, it was used in reference to divine intervention or appearances of the gods.

The appearance of grace has been uniquely instructive, showing us how to walk and talk. Negatively, it teaches us how to say "no" to ungodliness and worldly passion. Positively, it instructs us to ". . . live self-controlled, upright and godly lives in this present age" (Titus 2:12). Through the power of the Holy Spirit, we can now walk in a manner pleasing to God and "adorn" the message of salvation through Christ (Titus 2:10).

This does not mean that we are perfect. The instruction of grace is corrective in nature and assumes that we have many things to unlearn. Correction is our spiritual birthright as children of God, and we should not think that God is punishing us when He disciplines us in this way. If God did not correct us, it would suggest that we did not belong to Him (Hebrews 12:6–7). As we learn the lessons of grace that come to us as a result of Christ's first coming, we wait eagerly for another appearance: "the glorious appearing of our great God and Savior, Jesus Christ" (Titus 2:13). At His first coming, Christ was revealed in the humble form of a servant (Philippians 2:7). When He comes a second time, however, He will be revealed in glory. Furthermore, because He has purchased us for Himself, we will also be revealed with Him when He returns. We will share in His glory (Colossians 3:4).

Paul calls this expectation of Christ's return "the blessed hope" (Titus 2:13) Although this hope is focused on the future, it has very real implications for the present. One of the most practical is the perspective it gives concerning our current circumstances. The knowledge that God is using our daily experiences to train us helps us bear with uncomfortable situations because we know that when He comes, they will produce "an eternal glory that far outweighs them all" (2 Corinthians 4:17).

This hope of sharing in the glory of Christ provides the confidence we need to share the gospel boldly with others (2 Corinthians 3:12). It also motivates us to love other believers (Colossians 1:4–5). Its certainty is our motivation for godliness, which holds promise "for both the present life and the life to come" (1 Timothy 4:8).

Christians have often been criticized as being

"so heavenly minded that they are no earthly good." In reality, our "earthly good" lies precisely in the fact that we are heavenly minded. The one who has set his heart on the glory to be revealed in the church at the coming of Christ has a single ambition: to please Him (2 Corinthians 5:9). Whether at work, at home, or in the neighborhood, his every action works toward the single purpose of making Jesus Christ known.

The believer's greatest hope, however, is focused on the expectation that when Jesus Christ comes again, we will be His. This is far from what we once were. Before Christ called us to Himself, we were helpless (Romans 5:6). We were sinners (Romans 5:8). We were in the flesh and controlled by sinful passions (Romans 7:5). We were God's enemies (Romans 5:10). We were bound by the requirements of God's law but unable to fulfill those requirements, which made us no better than prisoners (Romans 7:6; Galatians 3:23). We were dead in our transgressions (Ephesians 2:5). This is no longer the case. Though we were once as worthless as Jarred's trophy, we have been purchased at a cost that is beyond calculation. Moreover, when God's transforming grace has completed its work, we will be displayed before all creation as trophies of grace, those who have been ransomed by blood and whose value is beyond measure.

Loving Savior, I look forward to the time when You come again and claim me as Your own. Until then, help me to view my current circumstances from a heavenly perspective. May I be a trophy of grace even now. Amen.

31

PARTAKERS OF CHRIST

> We have come to share in Christ if we hold firmly till the end the confidence we had at first. (*Hebrews 3:14*)

When the heart fails, it often takes the rest of the body with it. An ailing heart can place stress on other important organs, causing the kidneys, liver, or lungs to fail. In such cases, the body's natural responses work against itself, and functions that would otherwise be ordinary suddenly become deadly, so deadly, in fact, that even eating the wrong kind of sandwich can cause death! Sherwin B. Nuland, a professor of medicine and medical history at Yale University, describes such a case when he tells of a man who died of "acute pastrami-generated heart failure."

Fortunately, heart problems can often be diagnosed and treated with a combination of medicine and exercise. But what about ailments of the heart that are spiritual in nature? How can they be diagnosed and treated? The author of Hebrews describes just such a condition when he warns: "See to it, brothers, that none of you has a sinful, unbelieving heart that turns away from the living God" (Hebrews 3:12).

Like most heart disease, a "spiritual heart attack" can be recognized by its symptoms. The writer describes a process of spiritual decline, beginning with the deceitfulness of sin (Hebrews 3:13). The heart is hardened by the fraudulent appeal of sin, which challenges the limits that have been set by God. Once hardened, the heart "turns away from the living God." This is sometimes called apostasy, a term used to describe the rebellion of those who at one time professed to be followers of Christ but finally reject Him. The apostle Paul warned that the last days would be marked by a great falling away from Christ. According to 2 Thessalonians 2:1–4, the second coming of Christ will be preceded by a great "rebellion" and the appearance of the "man of lawlessness," or Antichrist.

The writer of Hebrews compares this kind of falling away to the rebellion of those Israelites who came out of Egypt in the Exodus and refused to enter Canaan (Hebrews 3:7–11). When Israelite spies came back and reported that the cities of Canaan were well fortified and their inhabitants powerful, God's people attacked the leadership of Moses and Aaron. Even worse, they questioned the goodness of God, saying: "Why is the Lord bringing us to this land only to let us fall by the sword? Our wives and children will be taken as plunder. Wouldn't it be better for us to go back to Egypt?" (Numbers 14:3). As a result, they were not permitted to enter the land until that entire generation died in the wilderness. Only Joshua and Caleb, who had believed God's promise, were allowed to go in with the second generation, after forty years of wandering in the wilderness.

The original readers of this epistle faced a simi-

lar temptation. Because they were originally from a
Jewish background, many had suffered persecution
when they identified themselves as followers of Jesus Christ. They had been insulted publicly,
imprisoned, and even had their property confiscat-
ed (Hebrews 10:34). Others were finding it hard to
accept the loss of centuries of tradition embodied
in the religious rituals that were now made obsolete
by Christ's sacrifice.

Their real problem was a crisis of confidence.
The writer points out the importance of faith in
God's promises by warning that only those who
hold their confidence firmly to the end show that
they have come to share in Christ (Hebrews 3:14).
It is important to understand that this is not a question of self-confidence but one of confidence in
Christ. Some Christians are so aware of their own
sinfulness that they struggle with doubts about
whether Christ will receive them. But Jesus has
promised: "All that the Father gives me will come
to me, and whoever comes to me I will never drive
away" (John 6:37). Other Christians question
whether they have enough faith. They have genuinely trusted in Christ, but they are afraid that
their faith is not large enough. According to Jesus,
though, faith that is as small as a mustard seed, as
long as it is genuine faith, is powerful enough to
move mountains (Matthew 17:20). It is the gen-
uineness of faith, rather than the amount, that is
important.

Those warned by the author of Hebrews had a
deeper problem. They had begun to question
whether Christ's blood was really all that they had
been told. Some were even considering turning

their backs on Christ and returning to the sacrificial system of Judaism (Hebrews 10:23–29). These people were in danger of rejecting Christ's sacrifice as the payment for their sin (Hebrews 10:29).

The writer uses a conditional sentence to emphasize the danger of such a choice, but he reverses the normal order. A typical conditional sentence consists of two parts. The first half of the sentence is the condition, while the second half is the result. For example, I might say: "If you invest wisely you will have money when you retire." If the condition is met, the result will be true. However, in Hebrews 3:14, the result rather than the condition is first.

By changing the normal order, the author does two things. First, he emphasizes the condition, drawing a subtle distinction in the order of the events of salvation. We must be in Christ in order to persevere in faith. It is faith rather than perseverance that comes first. He also indicates that perseverance in faith is diagnostic, that is, it serves as proof that one is truly a partaker of Christ.

The author's fear was that some who had claimed to be followers of Jesus had not truly placed their trust in Him as Christ. If it sounds like the writer is trying to get his readers to question their salvation, in a sense he is. The generation that perished in the wilderness came to the very edge of embracing God's promise but never crossed over. They wanted what God had to offer but on their own terms. When it comes to God's promises, however, it is God's way or no way.

Reversing the order of the condition in Hebrews 3:14 places the emphasis where it belongs: on Christ rather than on the believer. If it is true that only those who persevere in faith are partakers of Christ, then it is equally true that only those who are partakers in Christ can persevere in faith. It is Christ who makes the difference.

In the physical realm, hardening of the heart can be treated with medicine. If that is unsuccessful, the surgeon may go in and literally scrape out the arteries. Spiritual hardening of the heart, on the other hand, must be treated by exhortation. We are to ". . . encourage one another daily, as long as it is called Today, so that none of you may be hardened by sin's deceitfulness" (Hebrews 3:13).

Heavenly Father, grant me the gift of faith that comes as a result of Your loving grace. Show me the value of Christ's work. Help me never to take it for granted. Amen.

32

THOSE WHO ARE
WAITING FOR CHRIST

Just as man is destined to die once, and
after that to face judgment, so Christ was
sacrificed once to take away the sins of many
people; and he will appear a second time,
not to bear sin, but to bring salvation to those
who are waiting for him. *(Hebrews 9:27–28)*

The mound of freshly turned dirt looked like a
scar. It swelled above the grave with a starkness
that was painful to see. The wreaths that had been
gently placed there by the previous day's mourners
looked now as if they had been scattered in careless
haste. My little boy stood next to me, happily playing with one of the flowers that trailed from the
grave. He seemed oblivious to the surroundings,
but I was disturbed by the sight—not only because
it reminded me of the loss of my father, whose cas-
ket lay beneath, but because of the blunt proof it
offered of death's inevitability.

It is appointed to us to die. We may be able to
delay the onset of death for a time, but ultimately
we cannot avoid it. This alone would not be so bad,
if the cessation of physical life was all that we faced.
Then, at least, we could look at the prospect of
death through the eyes of the philosopher, who
suggested: "Give place to others, as others have giv-
en place to you." We might see death as the natural
culmination of life, as inevitable and peaceful as the
night's sleep that follows a hard day's work. But

while death may be normal, it is not natural. We rebel against the thought of death because inwardly we recognize it to be an intruder, robbing us of the birthright of eternal life, which was once ours before the fall.

Death is the tragic heritage of all those who are descended from Adam. It came into the world as a consequence of Adam's sin. When Adam fell, the twin curse of sin and death fell upon the entire human race (Romans 5:12–14).

In the Bible, death is portrayed as much more than a physical state. Ultimately, it is a spiritual reality: "As for you, you were dead in your transgressions and sins, in which you used to live when you followed the ways of this world and the ruler of the kingdom of the air, the spirit who is now at work in those who are disobedient" (Ephesians 2:1–2).

Before Jesus Christ gave us life, we were the living dead—dead in sin but living in transgressions and sins. This does not necessarily mean that we were pursuing a life of immorality and debauchery. It is possible to be very moral and still be spiritually dead. Indeed, one of the primary symptoms of spiritual death is the desire to justify oneself before God on the basis of human effort, rather than resting in the work of Christ. The writer of Hebrews refers to these human efforts as "dead works" (Hebrews 9:14 NASB, KJV). Since even our best efforts fall short of God's standard, a works-based approach to restoring our relationship with God is doomed to failure.

Some say that the fear of death is the fear of the unknown, but the opposite is actually the case. The real terror of death lies in what it says about us.

Physical death is a divine messenger bearing testimony to our need for forgiveness. Like Cain's mark, it is a perpetual reminder of our sin and of our alienation from God. It leaves us with irrefutable proof that even if we were somehow to do the impossible and climb by our own strength into the very presence of God, we would find the gates of heaven shut against us and the entrance barred forever.

Death results in the cessation of physical life, but it does not mean the end of our existence. It is appointed to us to die, but we also have an appointment with judgment (Hebrews 9:27). If we are to be judged on the basis of our merits, then condemnation must be our final sentence (Revelation 20:11–15). That is why the fear of death leaves us feeling like one who has been enjoying himself at the table just long enough to forget that the waiter is coming with the check. He knows that his wallet is empty and his credit card is going to be rejected because he hasn't been able to make the payments.

Fortunately, God has intervened on our behalf. Jesus Christ was "sacrificed once" to take away our sin. Unlike the sacrifices of the Old Testament Law, which could only prefigure Christ but not truly take away sin, the death of Jesus did not need to be repeated. Offered once for all time, the sacrifice of Christ is the only payment God will accept for sin. God's bill for our sin was presented to Jesus, and He paid it in full.

When Jesus came the first time, it was not to live so much as it was to die. Our Lord approached the grave with the relentless determination of a fighter stepping into the ring. He faced Satan, who had used the fear of death to enslave us, and disarmed him using the devil's own weapon (Hebrews 2:14–15).

Does this mean that a true Christian will never be afraid of death? Not necessarily. It is possible to know Christ and still find that the approach of death brings fear rather than comfort. There are many reasons for this. We may be more afraid of the process of dying than of death itself. Or we may fear losing those who will be separated from us. Whatever our fears, we can be certain that when we finally come to the place of death, Jesus will meet us there. He knows what it is like to stand at the graveside of a friend and mourn (John 11:35). He also knows what it is like to watch the approach of one's own death with a growing sense of apprehension (Luke 22:44). But by submitting to death Himself, Jesus made certain that those who belong to Him would be gloriously resurrected. Because of this, we look forward to Christ's second coming. When Jesus returns, He will not come to accomplish salvation but to bestow it. Death, referred to by the apostle Paul as the "last enemy," will itself be done away with, and we will be given an imperishable body (1 Corinthians 15:26, 49).

The grave that once seemed so scarred to me is now covered with grass. When I return to it, I cannot help thinking of the form that lies beneath and feeling a measure of grief. Each time, though, I remind myself that what lies buried there is not my father but the dwelling place he once inhabited. As one who had placed his faith in Christ's saving work, he is now in heaven with all those who, like me, are waiting for Christ's return.

Resurrected Lord, I place my hope in You and look forward to Your return. I know that when You come, my redemption will be complete. Amen.

33

A HOLY PRIESTHOOD

> As you come to him, the living Stone—
> rejected by men but chosen by God and
> precious to him—you also, like living
> stones, are being built into a spiritual house
> to be a holy priesthood, offering spiritual
> sacrifices acceptable to God through Jesus
> Christ. *(1 Peter 2:4–5)*

We usually refer to the place of worship as "our church." It is easy to see why. We fill its seats and attend its services. Its ministries are directed toward our needs. We pay the utility bills and see to it that its upkeep is maintained. The temple in Jerusalem, however, was different. Although God's people were allowed to worship in the temple courts, the temple itself was not constructed for them. When King David originally envisioned the temple, he saw it as a dwelling place for the ark of God (2 Samuel 7:2). David was not permitted to build the temple. Instead, his son Solomon was appointed by God to accomplish this task (2 Samuel 7:13; 1 Kings 6:12).

The temple, like the tabernacle that preceded it, was served by a team of priests. This calling, however, was not open to all Israelites. Only those who came from the tribe of Levi and were the descendants of Moses' brother Aaron could serve in this capacity (Deuteronomy 10:8). The priests examined the sacrifices of the people to make certain that they were acceptable and offered the sacrifices on the altar (Leviticus 1:7; 3:13). The remainder of the Levites assisted the priests and tended to the furnishings of worship (Numbers 1:50; Ezra 3:8).

We have a vivid example of the exclusivity of the priesthood in the Old Testament account of King Uzziah of Judah. In the ancient world, a king ruled with almost absolute power and could do just about anything he pleased. However, when Uzziah decided to offer incense in the temple, a privilege that belonged to the priests, he was opposed by God Himself (2 Chronicles 26:19).

Not every priest was permitted to enter the Holy of Holies where the ark of the Covenant was kept. This was reserved for the high priest alone, and he was only allowed to go in once a year, on the Day of Atonement. On that day, the high priest made offerings first for himself and then for the nation as a whole (Leviticus 16:2–6). He cast lots and selected one of two goats to offer as a sacrifice. The goat, which was referred to as the "scapegoat," was not sacrificed, but was driven into the wilderness (Leviticus 16:10). The term *scapegoat* comes from the Latin translation of the Old Testament, known as the Vulgate, and it originally had the sense of the "escape" goat. The scapegoat symbolized God's power to remove sins.

Once the scapegoat was driven into the wilderness, the high priest moved on to the most solemn part of the ceremony: passing through the veil that separated the Holy Place from the Holy of Holies. He did this three times. The first time, he offered incense (Leviticus 16:12–13). The second time, he offered the blood of a bull for himself and his family (Leviticus 16:14). The final trip was to offer the blood of the first goat that had not been driven into the wilderness on behalf of the congregation (Leviticus 16:15).

The New Testament explains that these restrictions were intended to signify the need for a mediator between God and humanity:

> *The Holy Spirit was showing by this that the way into the Most Holy Place had not yet been disclosed as long as the first tabernacle was still standing. This is an illustration for the present time, indicating that the gifts and sacrifices being offered were not able to clear the conscience of the worshiper.* (Hebrews 9:8–9)

First Peter 2:4–5 reveals that a radical change has taken place in the organization of worship with the coming of Christ and the establishment of the church. Now every believer functions as a priest. Access into the presence of God is no longer limited to a very few (Ephesians 2:18; 3:12). God's people now serve as both priesthood and temple combined.

There are certain groups within Christendom who assign the title of "priest" to those who lead them in worship. Others who reject this tradition follow it in practice when they hire pastoral staff and take no personal responsibility for the quality of the church's worship. In reality, however, every Christian shares this responsibility.

Like the priests who served under the Law of Moses, the church's believer priests also offer sacrifices. The church's offerings, however, are "spiritual sacrifices." Although different in form, they share a number of features in common with the sacrifices made under the Law of Moses. The offerings made under the Law could not take away sin, but were tangible sermons designed to point out the need for Christ (Hebrews 10:3–4). In the same way, the church's spiritual sacrifices cannot take away sin, but are made acceptable to God by the offering of Jesus Christ.

The sacrifices of the Mosaic Law looked forward to a redemption that was yet to be completed. The spiritual sacrifices of the church, on the other hand, look back to a redemption that has already been purchased. Both were based upon the hope of forgiveness in Christ. For those of the Old Testament, it was a hope promised. For those who have received Christ, it is a hope realized.

Like the temple at Jerusalem, the church does not exist for itself. We are both the dwelling place of God and His priests. This calling means that we have a responsibility whenever the church meets. It implies that the quality of worship in the congregation depends as much upon those who sit in the pews as it does upon the one who stands behind the pulpit. Worship is to be our calling, not our hobby.

Holy Spirit, help me to worship in spirit and in truth whenever the church is gathered together. Accept the spiritual sacrifices that I offer in Jesus' name. Amen.

34

A HOLY NATION

> But you are a chosen people, a royal
> priesthood, a holy nation, a people belong-
> ing to God, that you may declare the praises
> of him who called you out of darkness into
> his wonderful light. *(1 Peter 2:9)*

The church was not the first body of believers to
be called a "holy nation." This title was originally assigned to the nation of Israel soon after the
Exodus, while God's people were camped in the
wilderness of Sinai, near the mountain where
Moses received the Law of God. Although this was
not their final destination, it was a necessary pre-
liminary. After being rescued from slavery in Egypt
by the saving work of God, it was important that
the people of Israel learn about the God who had
saved them.

The Lord began by reminding the Israelites of
their changed status. They had previously been the
slaves of the Egyptians, but now they were God's
personal possession:

> *You yourselves have seen what I did to Egypt, and how I
> carried you on eagles' wings and brought you to myself.
> Now if you obey me fully and keep my covenant, then
> out of all the nations you will be my treasured posses-
> sion. Although the whole earth is mine, you will be for
> me a kingdom of priests and a holy nation. (Exodus
> 19:4–6).*

Two important truths were conveyed in this passage. The first truth is that God owns what He saves. This theme is echoed in the New Testament, where we read that those who receive salvation through Jesus Christ belong to God: "Do you not know that your body is a temple of the Holy Spirit, who is in you, whom you have received from God? You are not your own; you were bought at a price. Therefore honor God with your body" (1 Corinthians 6:19–20).

The second truth is that God's ownership obligates His people to obey. It is here, however, that we see an important difference between the law and the gospel. In Exodus 19:5–6, obedience was the condition of the relationship. The formula of the law is: "If you obey me fully . . . then you will be . . ." In the gospel, this perspective is reversed. In the Christian life, obedience is the result of salvation. Obedience is as important to God under the gospel as it was under the Law of Moses, but the basic difference between the two is that the gospel also provides what the Law demands. Peter's assertion that those who know Christ are a holy nation belonging to God is framed in unconditional language because the condition has already been met for them by Christ.

Peter's use of the language of Exodus 19:6 underscores the unique position of the church. Although God continues to have a purpose for the nation of Israel, it is currently suffering from what the apostle Paul characterizes as a temporary "hardening in part." This hardening will last until "the full number of the Gentiles has come in" (Romans 11:25). Once this has been accomplished, there will be a great turning to Christ among those who are the descendants of Abraham. God's purpose in allowing this hardening was not to exclude Israel from salvation but to establish grace as the only foundation for salvation: "For God has bound all men over to disobedience so that he may have mercy on them all" (Romans 11:32).

This desire to see both Jew and Gentile turn to Christ is reflected in the church's role as a preaching community. As a holy nation of people belonging to God, the church has been called to "declare the praises of him who called you out of darkness into his wonderful light" (1 Peter 2:9). Worship is only half of the church's work. We are to worship *and* proclaim. The Greek term that is translated "declare" in this verse refers to a solemn, public announcement.

Much has been said about the church's need to market itself to unbelievers. Some churches do this through advertising campaigns and scientific research. Others are more informal about the process. But most churches engage in some kind of marketing. We tell others how friendly our church is and describe the programs it offers. We plan special services to provide strangers with an incentive for visiting. These are all helpful, but it is important to recognize that ultimately it is not the church that we are to be marketing so much as it is God Himself. We are to be declaring God's "praises" or, more literally, His "excellencies." This term refers both to God's character and His acts.

People can learn about God by seeing His character reflected in us. This is why Peter stresses our position as a "holy nation." The church is holy because it has been set apart by God as the object of His loving grace. God's people also have a right to this title as those who reflect God in their behavior. Through the transformation of our lives by the Holy Spirit, we put a face on the invisible God for those who do not know Him.

In this respect, every believer is a walking billboard and cannot help saying something about Christ. We must ask ourselves, however, whether the message we bear is an accurate reflection of the gospel. The fact that we have been called "out of darkness into his wonderful light" suggests that the difference between those who know Christ and those who do not should be as radical as the difference between night and day.

The words Peter uses to describe the church in this verse do not tell us what we are to do but what we already are in Christ. Israel was commanded to live up to this standard but could not. The Gentiles were left to devise such a standard on their own but did not. It is Christ alone who can make us a holy nation.

Father, enable me to declare Your praise to those around me today, both in speech and action. Fill me, Holy Spirit, so that I may reflect my true status as part of a holy nation. Amen.

35

ALIENS AND STRANGERS

> Dear friends, I urge you, as aliens and
> strangers in the world, to abstain from sinful
> desires, which war against your soul. Live
> such good lives among the pagans that,
> though they accuse you of doing wrong,
> they may see your good deeds and glorify
> God on the day he visits us. *(1 Peter 2:11–12)*

The British author Horace Walpole wrote to a
friend about his visit to another country: "What
strikes me the most upon the whole is the total difference of manners between them and us, from the
greatest object to the least. There is not the smallest
similitude in the twenty-four hours. It is obvious in
every trifle."

Like Walpole, those who visit another culture
quickly become aware of how it is different from
their own. The Christian, however, faces this wher-
ever he or she goes. Those who belong to Christ are
"aliens and strangers" in the world. The term *aliens*
refers to someone without rights or legal status. In
biblical culture, as in our own, an alien was someone who holds his or her citizenship elsewhere.
The second term, *strangers,* has a slightly different
stress. It emphasizes the temporary nature of one's
residence and is sometimes translated "pilgrim."

Similar language was used of God's Old Testament people, Israel. For example, because God's
people were considered tenants in the Land of

Promise, a family could sell its property only temporarily: "The land must not be sold permanently, because the land is mine and you are but aliens and my tenants" (Leviticus 25:23). King David, like his ancestor Abraham, saw himself as a "stranger" (Psalm 39:12; cf. Hebrews 11:9).

Peter, however, uses these terms in a slightly different sense. Israel was a nation of aliens and pilgrims because the land belonged to God. But Peter describes the church in this way because its abiding home is with Christ. We are resident aliens because our true citizenship lies in heaven (Philippians 3:20). When the philosopher Diogenes was asked what country he was from, he replied: "I am a citizen of the world." The Christian would reply, "I am a citizen of the kingdom of heaven."

In 1 Peter 2:12, the apostle uses even stronger language and says that as pilgrims of Christ, we are living among "the pagans." This Greek term is one that literally means "the nations." It was the technical term used for those who were not the descendants of Abraham. In this way, Peter compares the church's position in the world to that of the Jews who had been scattered among the Gentiles.

What does it mean to live as aliens? One distinctive has to do with speech patterns. An alien often speaks a different language. This is also true of believers. Those who belong to Christ speak the language of edification. Our conversation is marked by ". . . only what is helpful for building others up according to their needs, that it may benefit those who listen" (Ephesians 4:29).

Aliens may also stand out from native residents

because of the way they dress. Like those of many other nations, God's people also have a distinctive costume. They wear the belt of truth, the breast-plate of righteousness, the footwear of the gospel, the helmet of salvation, and the sword of God's truth (Ephesians 6:14–17). In addition, they are to clothe themselves with humility (1 Peter 5:5).

A third characteristic of an alien is that his affections are tied to the mother country. He may be living in another country out of necessity or out of choice, but his true "home" is elsewhere. Likewise, we are told to "Set your minds on things above, not on earthly things" (Colossians 3:2).

When Peter describes the lifestyle of the pilgrim who follows Christ, he does so in both negative and positive terms. Negatively, we are to "abstain from sinful desires." This implies something important about the character of the believer. It suggests that such desires may continue to pose a problem, even after conversion. This is what the Bible calls the realm of "the flesh," a reference not to the skin that covers our bodies but to the principle that controlled our lives when we were alienated from God. Those who are "in the flesh" are in conflict with God. This is because ". . . the sinful mind is hostile to God. It does not submit to God's law, nor can it do so. Those controlled by the sinful nature cannot please God" (Romans 8:7–8).

Because the sinful nature of the Christian sees the soul as disputed territory, from time to time it will create a power struggle within us. When this happens, we find ourselves drawn toward an attitude or action that as Christians we would not normally consider. Our mind, aware of what the

Scriptures have to say, is horrified at the thought. Yet there is another part of us that is enticed. Something deep within us is ready, willing, and able to sin.

In the middle ages, some well-meaning but misguided Christians thought that the best way to deal with the flesh was to abuse the physical body. They would wear rough clothing, endure long fasts, and, in some cases, punish their bodies with whips. The theory behind such practices was that as the physical body became weaker, the flesh would lose its power. They quickly learned otherwise. Unfortunately, the flesh never loses its innate strength. It is as vital a force today in us as it was before we were born again. There is only one power strong enough to keep the flesh in check: "Those who belong to Christ Jesus have crucified the sinful nature with its passions and desires" (Galatians 5:24).

We are to be wise to the flesh and its tricks. The only way to live as pilgrims of Christ is to reject the way of the flesh and choose the path of the Spirit. When the sinful nature presents itself as a friend, we are to respond to it as an enemy and put it to death by yielding to the cross of Christ.

In positive terms, on the other hand, living as a pilgrim of Christ means that we will "Live such good lives among the pagans that, though they accuse you of doing wrong, they may see your good deeds and glorify God on the day he visits us" (1 Peter 2:12). Unfortunately, slander often comes with the calling of being a pilgrim for Christ. In many cases, those who do not know Christ have already passed judgment on us before they have heard a word of our message. The only way to counter such talk is by living a life worthy of the claims of the gospel. Notice, however, that in doing so our aim should not be our own vindication. In the end, it does not matter what others think of us. The only thing that counts is what others think of Christ.

A German prince who was known to be a great traveler offered the following advice to others who planned to follow in his steps: "In Naples, treat the people brutally; in Rome, be natural; in Austria, don't talk politics; in France, give yourself no airs; in Germany, a great many; and in England, don't spit." Peter's advice to travelers in this life is somewhat different. He urges us to live as aliens and strangers, glorifying God in all that we do. On the day of visitation, there will be vindication, not only of us, but of God Himself and the Christ we follow.

Holy Spirit, show me how to live the kind of life that will bring glory to Christ on the day of visitation. Amen.

36
CHRISTIANS

> If you suffer, it should not be as a murderer
> or thief or any other kind of criminal, or even
> as a meddler. However, if you suffer as a
> Christian, do not be ashamed, but praise God
> that you bear that name. *(1 Peter 4:15–16)*

Those who followed Jesus were first called "Christians" at Antioch (Acts 11:26). Apparently, those who heard the disciples refer to Jesus as Christ took it to be a personal name. They then added a Latin suffix that signified partisanship and called Christ's disciples "Christians." In the same way, those who followed Herod were known as "Herodians." The fact that some who were called by this name were embarrassed by it suggests that the title of "Christian" was originally used in ridicule. Moreover, Peter's statement that it was possible to suffer "as a Christian" implies that it was also potentially dangerous to be identified as a follower of Christ.

Tertullian, a Christian leader who lived in the third century, wrote that he and his fellow believers were often accused of being incestuous, and of killing infants, practicing atheism, and speaking treasonously against the emperor. Most of these accusations were the result of a misunderstanding of Christian doctrine and practices. For example, since all believers were regarded as "brothers" and "sisters" in Christ, including those who were married to one another, some falsely concluded that incest was a common practice in the church. The charge of infanticide may have come from a misunderstanding of the nature of the work of the Cross and its power to "put to death" the old nature. Because Christians rejected the polytheism of the Roman empire and held that there was only one true God, they were regarded as "atheists." And their refusal to pay homage to the emperor, who claimed to be divine, led to the charge of treason and sometimes resulted in death.

According to 1 Peter 4:12–13, we should expect these kinds of accusations: "Dear friends, do not be surprised by the painful trial you are suffering, as though something strange were happening to you. But rejoice that you participate in the suffering of Christ, so that you may be overjoyed when his glory is revealed."

Some Christians feel outraged when they go through trials simply because they are Christians. They can understand how such things might happen to those who have turned their backs on Christ, but not to a true disciple. These believers are like the troubled saint who once complained: "If this is how God treats His friends, no wonder He has so few of them."

Peter's response to this complaint is somewhat surprising. Instead of defending God, he states that such experiences are common to believers. What is more, he commands us to rejoice when such things occur. Fortunately, he also tells us how such a response is possible. The secret to enduring such circumstances joyfully is to draw a line from our suffering to Christ. The closer the connection, the greater our joy will be.

Peter, however, is no masochist. He is not saying, "Enjoy your suffering." The real source of joy is not the suffering itself but that our suffering is related to Christ. The joy Peter speaks of in this verse is a rejoicing in the privilege of being allowed to suffer on Christ's behalf, rather than in the experience of pain. Peter knew this kind of joy firsthand. The mature Christian rejoices because he or she has been allowed, in some measure, to follow Christ's example and to reflect His glory: "If you are insulted because of the name of Christ, you are blessed, for the Spirit of glory and of God rests on you" (1 Peter 4:14).

Peter tells us that we are to rejoice when we suffer for Christ. Some of the suffering we endure, however, may be of our own making (1 Peter 4:15). At times, the accusations that others make of Christians are rooted in truth. How often have we heard someone respond to our presentation of the gospel with the words, "I used to know someone who believed like you do, and they. . . ."

When people and circumstances turn against us, our first response should be to examine our own actions in order to see if we bear any of the responsibility for our suffering. Have we unnecessarily offended others? Is our suffering the consequence of our own disobedient choices? Some believers look at the wreck and ruin of their lives and ask God why He allowed such a thing to happen, when in reality they have only themselves to blame. Not all suffering is a cause for rejoicing. Some who are miserable deserve to be miserable. In such cases, suffering may actually be God's way of getting our attention and drawing us back to Himself. The Bible, however, is full of accounts of men and women who made foolish choices but by God's grace were allowed to rebuild their lives.

When we suffer as Christians, we suffer because of who we are, not because of what we have done. Indeed, we may actually be suffering because of something that God is doing. In 1 Peter 4:17 the apostle characterizes the sufferings of the church as the beginning of God's judgment: "For it is time for judgment to begin with the family of God; and if it begins with us, what will the outcome be for those who do not obey the gospel of God?"

Scientists have known for some time that earthquakes produce tremors known as "aftershocks." Now they have discovered that there may also be tremors *before* the earthquake. Perhaps future scientific discoveries will enable them to use these tremors to predict when such events will occur.

In the same way, the church's sufferings are the "foreshocks" of a great judgment, serving as both a warning and an encouragement. For suffering believers, they offer encouragement. They are a reminder that God notes their suffering and will one day call everyone to account. If God uses the wicked to judge the church, He will certainly not let the wicked go free. To the world, the sufferings of the church provide a solemn warning: If God intends to deal with the sins of His own people, then those who have rejected Him cannot hope to escape.

The old saint who wondered why God treated his friends in such a way asked the wrong question. The real question is, "If God treats His friends this way, what will He do to His enemies?"

We suffer as Christians because we are allowed

the privilege of following Christ's example. We suffer because we are on the threshold of final judgment. But more than anything else, we suffer because we are Christians.

Suffering and Victorious Savior, help me to remember that it is a privilege to suffer as a Christian. Strengthen and encourage me in such times so that my response will bring glory to You on the day of visitation. Amen.

37
THE BRIDE OF CHRIST

> Let us rejoice and be glad and give him
> glory! For the wedding of the Lamb has
> come, and his bride has made herself ready.
> (*Revelation 19:7*)

The photograph on my wall is of a young bride.
Her eyes sparkle as she rests her head on the
groom's shoulder and smiles shyly. Her face is
wreathed in a bright veil and she is wearing a radiant gown. John provides us with a similar portrait
in Revelation 19:7. However, unlike my photograph, which captured a moment from the past and
preserved it for the future, John's picture frames an
event that is yet to take place. He is describing the
wedding of Jesus Christ to the church.

This biblical portrait of Christ's relationship to
the church is based upon the Jewish practice of betrothal and marriage. During the New Testament
era, the marriage process took place in three stages.
It began with the betrothal, usually arranged by the
bride's parents. The betrothal lasted for approxi-
mately a year and was regarded as being as binding
as the marriage itself. A woman who was betrothed
could be executed for adultery, and dissolving the
betrothal required a legal divorce. At the betrothal,
the woman received a gift from her future husband.
At the end of the betrothal period, the couple cele-
brated the wedding feast, a community-wide event

that would often last for several days. Following this, the newly married couple returned to the home of the groom's parents to live.

In the New Testament the church is portrayed as being in the betrothal period in its relationship to Jesus Christ. When John the Baptist was told that Jesus was baptizing a greater number of disciples than John was, he used the analogy of a wedding in his reply: "The bride belongs to the bridegroom. The friend who attends the bridegroom waits and listens for him, and is full of joy when he hears the bridegroom's voice. That joy is mine, and it is now complete" (John 3:29).

In the parable of the ten virgins, Jesus compared the kingdom of heaven to those who were waiting for the bridegroom to come and claim his bride (Matthew 25:1–13). Jesus' purpose in telling this parable was to warn His disciples of the need to be prepared for His coming.

Similarly, the apostle Paul saw himself as playing a role in the betrothal process of the bride of Christ. When the Corinthian church seemed in danger of being deceived by false teachers, Paul wrote: "I am jealous for you with a godly jealousy. I promised you to one husband, to Christ, so that I might present you as a pure virgin to him" (2 Corinthians 11:2).

We have been betrothed to Jesus Christ and are now waiting for Him to come and claim us as His own. We have received the Holy Spirit as a kind of betrothal gift, a seal that guarantees that we are Christ's (Ephesians 1:13; 4:30). During this betrothal period, however, we do not stand idly by as we wait for the appearance of the Bridegroom. Ac-

cording to Revelation 19:7, when Jesus Christ finally returns, He will find that "his bride has made
herself ready."

The bride in my photograph spent months
carefully selecting a gown. On the appointed day,
she arose early in the morning and began to prepare herself for the wedding. Like her, Christ's
bride will also be given a gown to wear. When Jesus
Christ comes He will find a church that has been
cleansed by His work and His Word, and who is
free of any stain, wrinkle, or blemish (Ephesians
5:25–27). He will also find that the church has prepared herself for His arrival. According to John, the
church's wedding gown is made of "the righteous
acts of the saints" (Revelation 19:8). While these
are genuinely the deeds of the saints, they flow out
of the work of Christ. They are righteous acts done
in the power of the Holy Spirit.

What is most striking about John's description
of the church in these verses is its tone of certainty.
These words are prophetic rather than didactic. He
is not telling us what we *should* be like but showing
us what we *will* be like when Christ comes to claim
His bride.

While there are many photographs that seem
to resemble the one that hangs on my wall, none of
them is quite like the one I referred to at the beginning of this chapter. It is unique in all the world in
this one respect: It is a portrait of *my* bride. Each
time I look at it I am reminded again that she is
mine alone, joined to me in Christ by a covenant of
love. I am also reminded that the love I feel for her
is, in some small way, a reflection of the love that
Jesus Christ has for His church. It is a visible token

of the event that John depicts in this text—the day when the heavenly Bridegroom will appear and will say to the church, "Arise, come, my darling; my beautiful one, come with me" (Song of Solomon 2:13).

Even so, come Lord Jesus! Amen.